Miniature
Embroidery
for the
Tudor & Stuart
Dolls' House

Miniature Embroidery

for the
Tudor & Stuart
Dolls' House

Pamela Warner

GUILD OF MASTER CRAFTSMAN PUBLICATIONS LTD

First published in 2001 by
Guild of Master Craftsman Publications Ltd,
166 High Street, Lewes,
East Sussex, BN7 1XU

Copyright © Guild of Master Craftsman Publications Ltd
Text copyright © Pamela Warner 2001

ISBN 1 86108 217 7

A catalogue record of this book is available from the British Library

Photography by Anthony Bailey,
except the following by Pamela Warner:
Figs 2.9, 2.10, 2.13, 2.14, 2.17, 2.23, 2.24, 2.25, 2.26, 2.27,
3.3, 3.7, 3.9, 3.15, 4.3, 4.4, 4.7, 4.11, 4.17, 4.18, 4.24, 5.6, 6.6.

Charts produced by Peter Rhodes

Black-and-white line drawings by John Yates, from sketches by Pamela Warner,
except drawings in the Stitch Glossary, by Pamela Warner

Colour drawings and patterns © Pamela Warner

Series design by Teresa Dearlove
Book edited and designed by Margot Richardson

All rights reserved

The right of Pamela Warner to be identified as the author of this work has been asserted in
accordance with the Copyright, Designs and Patents Act 1988, Sections 77 and 78.

No part of this publication may be reproduced, stored in a retrieval system
or transmitted in any form or by any means without the prior permission
of the publisher and copyright owner.

This book is sold subject to the condition that all designs are copyright and are not for
commercial production without the permission of the designer and copyright owner.

The publishers and author can accept no legal responsibility for any consequences arising
from the application of information, advice or instructions given in this publication.

Typeface: Perpetua

Colour origination by Viscan Graphics (Singapore)
Printed and bound by Kyodo Printing (Singapore) under the supervision of
MRM Graphics, Winslow, Buckinghamshire, UK

Contents

With thanks and love to my daughter Debi and my son Stephen.

Acknowledgements

Frames for the band and spot samplers by Adam Syred of Wood Supplies; all other furniture and frames by the author.

Note on Measurements

Throughout, measurements are given in both metric and imperial systems. Please use only one system for each project as the two are close alternatives only, not exact conversions.

All the projects contained in this book are presented to 1/12th scale.

A Tudor-style dolls' house is often the preferred choice for miniaturists and collectors. Many makers provide kits and ready-made houses, or specialize in furniture of this period. I have extended the range of this book to cover the seventeenth century, or Stuart period, mainly to enable me to include some of the delightful forms of embroidery that followed the styles of the Tudor reigns.

Almost any sizable museum with a textile collection will have a selection of sixteenth- and seventeenth-century embroideries. The richness and beauty of the work will be immediately apparent: coloured silk embroidery or blackwork intermingled with silver and gold; charming flowers buzzing with tiny insects; pastoral scenes and amusing naive animals; and stories and scenes worked in the technique known as stumpwork.

I have two Tudor-style houses in my collection. One is based on a large timbered country mansion, c. 1600, very late Elizabethan and furnished in the manner of 50 years after that date. The second house is a small jettied timber house, similar in style to 'the house that moved' in Exeter, England, now the Tourist Information centre. I have made my version longer, for more space, and it is to be a museum (housing some of the projects in this book). Another advantage of the period covered here is that the items could be placed in a house of any period, as though it were an heirloom handed down or an antique.

The previous two volumes in this series contain projects for the Victorian period, 1837–1910, and the Georgian era, 1702–1830. This volume is based on actual pieces from the middle of the sixteenth to the end of the seventeenth century. The projects have been designed for use by stitchers, many of whom will have some experience and for those who may be trying for the first time. The basic techniques are very simple; some projects just take longer.

I hope you experience many hours of pleasure creating 'little treasures' for your dolls' house, room box or simple display area.

Introduction

1 Influences on design and style

The projects in this volume are based on antique pieces dating from the middle of the sixteenth to the end of the seventeenth century. Although, strictly speaking, the Tudor period pre-dates this timescale, it was not until the reign of Elizabeth I that embroidery reached a prestigious height with many established workshops. The Elizabethan era heralded the second great period of English embroidery, the first being that of Opus Anglicanum, the magnificent church embroidery of the medieval period, when the main professional workshops were in London, Winchester and Ely.

During the Tudor period a time of prolonged peace came about resulting in great wealth for the aristocracy. This came from the expanding trade and voyages of discovery, resulting in a culture where many hours were spent in leisure and leading to a huge demand for beautiful costume and furnishings. A conspicuous display

DATE	MONARCH
Tudors	
1485–1509	Henry VII
1509–1547	Henry VIII
1547–1553	Edward VI
1553–1554	Jane
1553–1558	Mary I (ruled for nine days)
1558–1603	Elizabeth I
Stuarts	
1603–1625	James I (VI Scotland)
1625–1649	Charles I
1649–1659	Commonwealth
1660–1685	Charles II
1685–1688	James II (VII Scotland)
1689–1702	William III and Mary II
1702–1714	Anne

of wealth became desirable. The houses of the rich became more comfortable; the earlier large communal hall was reduced in size; many more individual rooms were introduced, each with a fireplace; internal staircases gave easy access; and larger glazed windows let in light.

When thinking of Tudor times, most of us focus on the timber-framed buildings which were found at all levels of society, from the humble dwellings of the poor, to large mansions in both town and country. Generally speaking, the more timbers used, the wealthier the occupier. However, buildings of granite, stone and red brick could also be found, with the use of brick and stone increasing in the seventeenth century. The gable ends of some very late seventeenth-century houses show a Dutch influence introduced by William III.

Fig 1.1 **The dominant scrolling stem design as used in the second half of the sixteenth century on costume and household items**

Fig 1.2 **The Lucretia's Banquet table carpet, late sixteenth century, showing the use of the strapwork design to divide the ground. Each compartment is then filled with a design**

The most important room in a wealthy household was the main bedroom, the bed being a prestigious piece of furniture hung with rich hangings. The head of the household would receive his visitors in the bedroom, giving him another opportunity to display his wealth. The structure of the bed could be very simple but the bed hangings would be sumptuous, the best that could be afforded. En suite with the bed would be a set of ten or twelve stools, each with a cushion.

A dominant design feature during the sixteenth century was the use of the scrolling stem (*see* Fig 1.1). This was a method of dividing the background into compartments, allowing each one to be filled with a plant, flower, insect or fruit motif. During Elizabeth's reign, these motifs would be varied with very little repetition. The same style continued into the early seventeenth century, but the motifs were often repeated, having less spontaneity.

A favourite device for the architects, sculptors and wood carvers of the time for decoration was known as strapwork (*see* Fig 1.2). This was copied by the embroiderers and used to create a framework in which to place motifs or pictorial scenes. Journeyman embroiderers and traders would travel around the country, calling at the houses of the wealthy, to sell materials to the ladies, and to prepare work for them. The designs were often selected from herbals and books, illustrated with woodcuts, that were available. The journeyman would mark the design on to the fabric, supply the threads and, sometimes, actually start the work to show how it should be done.

Much embroidery was produced in professional workshops. However, the prosperity and leisure time of the Elizabethan period resulted in a great deal of amateur work. All manner of items were embroidered and many techniques were used.

Canvaswork was a popular choice, used widely for cushions and, later, for chair covers, due to its durability. Canvaswork was also chosen for valances and pictures as the technique lends itself well to pictorial subjects. Many ladies used canvaswork if they were making larger items, such as bed or wall hangings, as the designs could be worked in small pieces and then assembled on a velvet or silk fabric (*see* Fig 1.3).

As already mentioned, embroidery in coloured or black silk was popular, often embellished with metal threads or spangles, tiny pierced discs of silver or gold sewn on in a similar manner to a modern sequin. In the seventeenth century some of the silk and metal embroidery became very raised, resulting in what was later called stumpwork.

Quilting was used for practical and costume items. However, at this early time, the patterns were quite plain. It was regarded as a primarily utilitarian method of sandwiching together fabrics for warmth.

The background to the various items, techniques and styles included in this volume is given in greater detail within the relevant chapters.

Fig 1.3 **Examples of canvaswork slips which would be applied to fabric to create larger items**

2 Bed hangings

The importance of the bed in Tudor and Stuart times has been mentioned in the previous chapter. Whereas the actual bed could be very basic, the sumptuous hangings were used to display the status and wealth of the owner. The value of such hangings could be greater than the entire contents of the rest of the house. The most highly treasured and sought-after fabrics were woven: imported silks, Venetian-figured or stamped silk velvets, and fabrics with a weft of silver or gold. Although embroidered bed hangings were produced in professional workshops, many surviving examples are the work of amateur needlewomen.

The items comprising a set of bed hangings for a four-poster bed (*see* Fig 2.1), were:

The tester: a decorated fabric or lining inside the 'roof' of the bed.

The headpiece: a decorated fabric hanging at the head of the bed, possibly with a headboard.

Curtains: two, four or six curtains. Two were used on a half-tester, or on a four-poster with ornately carved posts; while four or six curtains were arranged with one at each top corner and one or two at each post at the foot of the bed.

Valances, upper and lower: provided the best areas for decoration, particularly for pictorial themes. The lower valances hung from the mattress supports at the sides and foot of the bed, to floor level. The upper valances were hung from the top frame of the bed, sometimes in one continuous piece, or in separate sections for the sides and foot of the bed. Many upper valances have survived as they were not handled as much as the remaining hangings.

Stool cushions: a set of cushions for ten or twelve stools would complete the set.

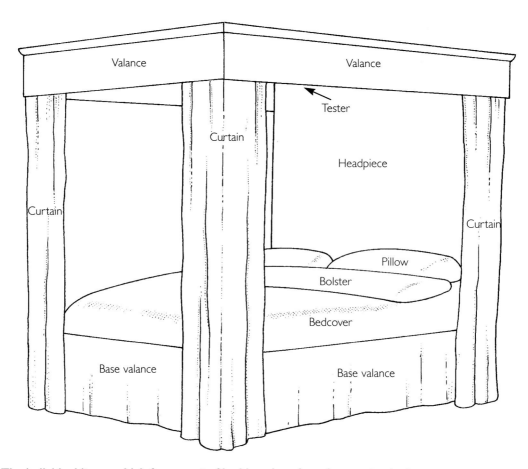

Fig 2.1 **The individual items which form a set of bed hangings for a four-poster bed**

A wide range of techniques were used by embroiderers for bed hangings:

Canvaswork allowed the worker, or group of workers, to produce small pieces which could then be applied to silk or velvet fabric to create the large items that form a set. This method was used in two main ways:

1 Circular, square, rectangular or cruciform pieces of canvaswork, often pictorial, could be worked on small embroidery frames. The pieces could range in size from 15–45/50cm (6–18/20in), being very easy to manage when in progress. The Oxburgh Hangings are a good example of this technique, although they have been remade at some later date. The surviving pieces can be seen at Oxburgh Hall, Oxborough, Norfolk, England, and in the Victoria and Albert

Museum in London. Many of the applied pieces include the ciphers of Mary Queen of Scots and Bess of Hardwick who, with help from their maids, worked the embroidery. The first project in this chapter (*see* page 12) is based on these hangings.

2 The second type of applied canvaswork was in the form of 'slips'. Instead of being pictorial shapes, as above, these were motifs selected from the herbals of the time: books of woodcuts illustrating plants and fruit. The motifs were copied directly from the books and worked with an outline of black tent or cross stitch, with the coloured details filled in. These pieces were then cut out in great detail, following the outline of the motif, and applied to the fabric background with a couched line around the edges. There are many surviving examples of this method, the most remarkable being a large collection of unused slips in Traquair House, Innerleithen, Peebleshire, Scotland. The second project (*see* page 17) is based on canvaswork slips.

Crewelwork was another widely used technique for bed hangings. It takes its name from the crewel wool used for the embroidery, a hard-wearing worsted wool. During the sixteenth century, designs were based on a scrolling stem as described on page 4. The stem formed compartments for all manner of flowers, fruit and insects. During the seventeenth century, the stem became more of a tree form, based on the 'tree of life' tradition. This was depicted growing from a little hill or mound, and as the century progressed the tree and the mound became more and more ornate and exotic, with fantasy birds and monkeys in the branches, and lions, unicorns, rabbits and mythological beasts around the base. The fourth project (*see* page 25) is based on a tree of life design.

Two contrasting crewelwork beds of note can be seen at Cotehele House in Cornwall, England. One is a tree of life design, the other a simple scrolling stem worked in red wool. The third project (*see* page 22) is based on this bed. An unusual and amusing version of a crewelwork design, showing individual motifs and exotic animals, worked by a young girl, Abigail Pett, can be seen in the Victoria and Albert Museum in London.

Given that woven silks were very highly prized, some bed hangings were simply decorated with embroidery and braids. Heraldic devices were a popular choice. Some beds had ornately carved headboards and cornices above the valance. The carved wood was covered with silk fabric and decorated with braids and tassels. A bed of this type, the Melville bed, can also be seen in the Victoria and Albert Museum. The fifth project (*see* page 29) is of this type.

Determining the size

Prior to the late nineteenth century, beds were not a standard size, being individually made for the occupant. Even the kits and ready-made miniature beds available will vary slightly in size and, certainly, in style. Therefore you will need to measure your particular bed to find the correct size for your bed hangings. To make paper patterns *see* Fig 2.2.

Headpiece: measure the width between the bedposts at the head of the bed (A–B). Then measure the height from just above the mattress to the top of the bed frame (G–B). Add 15mm (½in) all round the edges for turnings.

Tester: measure the width (A–B) and the length (A–C) of the bed inside the upper bed frame. Add 15mm (½in) all round the edges for turnings.

Upper valance: measure the length of the side of the bed to the outside of the upper bed frame (A–C), continue across the end of the bed (C–D) and along the other side (D–B). An upper valance can be between 25 and 30mm (1 and 1¼in) wide. Add 15mm (½in) turning along the top edge of the valance and a turning equal to the width of the valance along the lower edge.

The upper valance can be made in three separate pieces if desired, having a join at each corner. In this case, cut your pattern in a similar way to the lower valances using the top measurements.

Lower valances: measure the length of the bed between the bedposts (A–C). The height (E–F) is between the top of the mattress and the floor level. Add 15mm (½in) turning along the top edge and the height of the valance for the lower turning. Cut two pieces to these measurements.

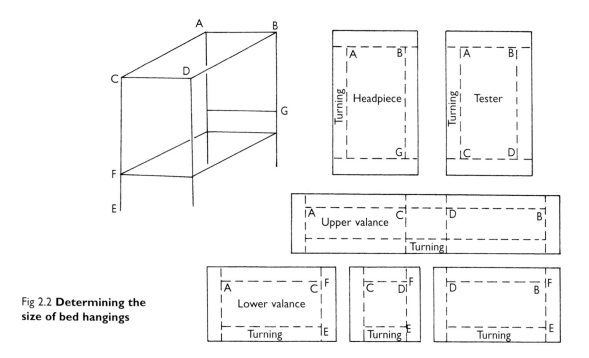

Fig 2.2 **Determining the size of bed hangings**

Measure the width of the bed (C–D) between the bedposts at the foot of the bed, height and turnings as above. Cut one piece.

Curtains: if the curtains are to be gathered or pleated, cut them about 75mm (3in) wide with a turning of 6mm (¼in) either side. Measure the height of the bed (C–E) to find the length of the curtains and add 6mm (¼in) turning at the lower edge for a hem.

Bedcovers

Instructions for making these are given in Chapter 3, pages 37–51.

Oxburgh Bed Hangings

The embroidery featured on the original Oxburgh Hangings dates from about 1570. The linen canvas panels were embroidered in coloured silk using cross stitch and applied to dark green velvet with a linking design of couched red cords.

They were worked by Mary Queen of Scots and Elizabeth, Countess of Shrewsbury (Bess of Hardwick) and the ladies of their household. The motifs were chosen from the books of the time and were worked as square, octagonal and cruciform shapes.

The square panel, for use on the headpiece or tester, shows blossom and fruit trees surrounded by a border of flowers, fruit and nuts (*see* Fig 2.5A). There are two octagonal panels, for use in the centre of the valances at the foot of the bed. One shows a fruit tree, the other, one of Mary Queen of Scots favourite emblems, the marigold turning from the sun, intimating that only a queen can look at the sun (*see* Figs 2.5B and 2.5C).

The 12 cruciform shapes include some of the amusing animals and birds that were chosen for the original hangings; a camel, elephant, crocodile, cat, unicorn, frogs, dolphin, phoenix, spider, cock, a pheasant (with the tail

Fig 2.3 **The Oxburgh bed (shown with the Scrolling Stem bedcover and pillow – see pages 39–41).**

Oxburgh Bed Hangings

Materials

Evenweave linen or cotton (32 count):

   4 curtains: 110 x 30cm (43 x 12in)

   2 curtains: 80 x 30cm (32 x 12in)

Stranded cotton as listed in colour key

Tapestry needle: No. 26

Tacking cotton

Sewing thread to match fabric or PVA fabric glue

Size

Square panel: 48 stitches square, 37mm (1⁷⁄₁₆in) square

Octagonal panels: 40 x 40 stitches, 30 x 30mm (1³⁄₁₆ x 1³⁄₁₆in)

Cruciform panels: 32 x 32 stitches, 25 x 25mm (1 x 1in)

Individual items as per pattern

conveniently cut in half to fit the shape) and, finally, a monkfish in the form of a monk with a fish's tail (*see* Fig 2.4). These can be used in whichever positions you prefer.

See also instructions for matching cushions (page 53) and a wall hanging (page 122).

Working method

Coloured evenweave linen was used for this project. A natural-coloured linen could be used, as for the chair cover in Chapter 5 (*see* page 68) and the three-fold screen in Chapter 6 (*see* page 81). You could colour white fabric as directed in Chapter 13 (*see* page 145), which should be done first.

1 Make paper patterns for all required pieces as directed above (*see* page 10). Note that the curtains for this bed hang as flat panels, which is seen on actual beds of this period. Some, however, may have had additional curtains behind the panels which would have been drawn when required. (The gathered curtains

were in addition to the flat ones, but are not possible for miniatures.) The density of the embroidery for this project would make it difficult to gather or pleat the curtains.

The narrow flat panels at the head of the bed are 33mm (1¼in) wide with 25mm (1in) turnings either side. The wider, folded panels for the foot of the bed are 64mm (2½in) wide with turnings as above (*see* Fig 2.4).

2 Using the paper patterns, mark the fabric with tacking stitches to show the outlines of each piece. Leave sufficient fabric between the pieces to allow for the turnings. Also mark with tacking stitches the horizontal and vertical centres of each piece (*see* page 140).

3 If all the above pieces have been marked up together on one piece of fabric, mount the fabric onto a rectangular stretcher frame, or place a ring frame on the area being worked. If the pieces have been marked up on separate pieces of fabric, mount each piece as required in a card mount. This process is described in Materials and working methods (*see* page 136).

13

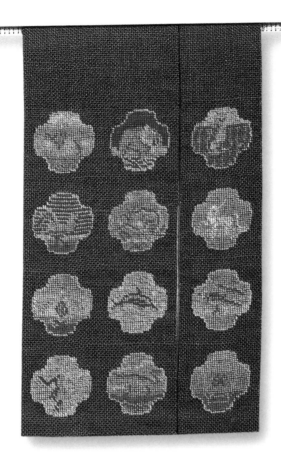

Fig 2.4 **The curtain panels for the Oxburgh bed**

Oxburgh Bed Hangings

		Skeins	DMC	Anchor	Madeira
	Gold	I	725	298	0106
	Light green	I	906	238	1410
	Dark green	I	904	239	1413
	Light fawn	I	437	362	2012
	Mid brown	I	435	365	2010
	Dark brown	I	801	359	2007
	Light blue	I	800	9159	1002
	Mid blue	I	813	140	1013
	Dark blue	I	797	133	0912
	Light pink	I	225	23	0510
	Dark pink	I	224	26	0813
	Light grey green	I	504	875	1701
	Dark grey green	I	502	877	1703
	Grey	I	451	235	1808
	Red	I	321	9046	0510
	White	I	Blanc	001	White

Fig 2.5A **Chart for the Oxburgh square panel**

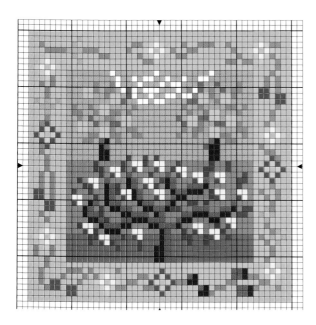

Fig 2.5B & C **Charts for the Oxburgh octagonal panels**

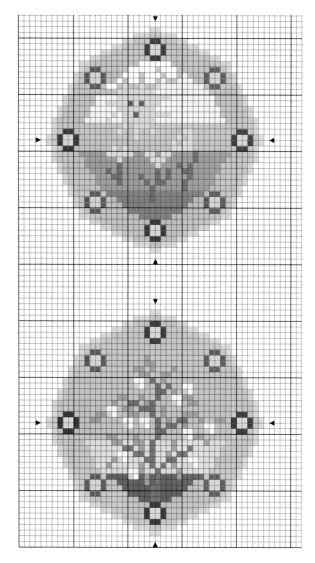

4 Refer to the charts (Figs 2.5A, 2.5B and 2.5C for the square and octagonal panels, Fig 2.6 for the wide curtain panels, and Fig 2.7 for the narrow curtain panels). Use one strand of stranded cotton and tent stitch throughout. When working the valances, place an octagonal motif in the centre and position the smaller motifs with 12 or 15 threads between. Place the square motif a little above the centre on the headpiece, or in the centre of the tester. Use the positions on the charts as a guide for the curtain panels. You may find it easier to work the outer edges first.

5 When the embroidery is complete, remove the fabric from the frame.

6 Check the measurements of the completed pieces against the bed as the upper valance is mounted outside the curtains and may need to be a little longer than expected.

7 Make up the hangings as shown on page 34.

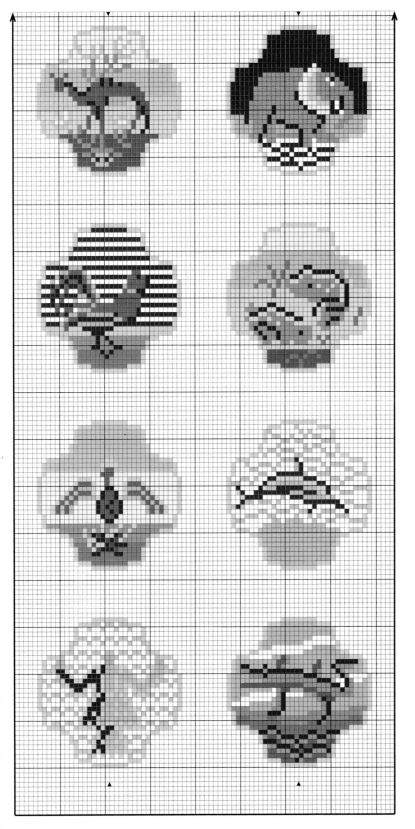

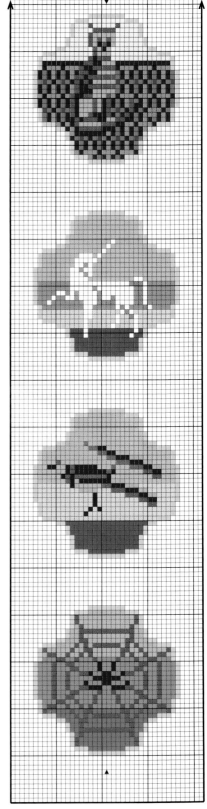

Fig 2.6 **Chart for the Oxburgh bed wide curtain**

Fig 2.7 **Chart for narrow curtain**

Fig 2.8 **The Slips bed (with the Gold Trellis bedcover and pillow – *see* page 45)**

Slips Bed Hangings

The use of slips was a great favourite of the embroiderers during the sixteenth and seventeenth centuries as it allowed them to work small pieces of canvaswork and assemble them into larger furnishing items. The word 'slip' is a gardening term for a cutting, and the designs were copied directly from the herbals and books of the period. The canvas used would, to our eyes, look more like an evenweave linen, not the stiffened canvas we know now.

The slips would have been worked in tent or cross stitch and cut around the detailed outlines leaving a small edge of the fabric showing. The piece was then applied to the desired fabric with a couched line of metal thread or silk.

See also instructions for making matching cushions (page 54), foot stool (page 71), screen (page 81), chair (page 71) and wall hanging (page 123).

Slips Bed Hangings

Materials

Evenweave linen or cotton (32 count):

    4 curtains: 110 x 30cm (43 x 12in)

    2 curtains: 80 x 30cm (32 x 12in)

Stranded cotton as listed in colour key

Tapestry needle: No. 26

Tacking cotton

Sewing thread to match fabric or PVA fabric glue

Size

Each motif: 28 stitches square, 20mm (¾in) square

Individual items as per pattern

Working method

Coloured evenweave linen was used for this project (*see* Figs 2.8 and 2.9). A natural-coloured linen (*see* Fig 2.10), could be used as for the screen (*see* page 81) and chair cover (*see* page 71). Alternatively, you may decide that you wish to colour your own fabric. (*See* Chapter 13, page 145).

1 Make paper patterns for all the required items as directed (*see* Fig 2.2, page 11). Note that the curtains for this project hang as flat panels, as on the Oxburgh Hangings. This is seen on some beds of this period which may have had additional gathered curtains under the panels. The density of the embroidery for this project would make it difficult to gather or pleat curtains on this scale.

The narrow flat panels at the head of the bed are 33mm (1¼in) wide with 25mm (1in) turnings either side. Wider, folded panels for the foot of the bed can be made (*see* Oxburgh Hangings), and would be 64mm (2½in) wide with turnings as above.

Fig 2.9 **Motifs for the Slips bed**

18

Fig 2.10 **The motifs on a
lighter ground**

2 Using the paper patterns, mark the fabric with tacking stitches to show the outlines of each piece. Leave sufficient fabric between the pieces to allow for the turnings. Also mark with tacking stitches the horizontal and vertical centres of each piece (*see* page 140: photograph showing a piece marked).

3 If all the pieces have been marked up together on one piece of fabric, mount the fabric into a rectangular stretcher frame, or place a ring frame on the area to be worked. If the pieces have been marked on separate pieces of fabric, mount each piece as required in a card mount. This process is described in Materials and working methods (*see* page 136).

4 Refer to chart (*see* Fig 2.11) to select the motifs. These can be placed in any order you prefer. Use one strand of stranded cotton and tent stitch throughout. When working the valances, begin by placing one motif in the centre and spacing additional motifs either side with 10 or 12 threads between, to the desired length. For a headpiece or tester, work a group of four motifs in the centre. For curtains, space the motifs above one another, working from the bottom hem, leaving 10 or 12 threads between the motifs.

5 When the embroidery is complete, remove the fabric from the frame.

6 Check the measurements of the completed pieces against the bed as the upper valance is mounted outside the curtains and may need to be a little longer than expected.

7 Make up the hangings as shown on page 34.

19

Slips Bed Hangings

		Skeins	DMC	Anchor	Madeira
	Dark blue	I	797	147	0912
	Mid blue	I	799	145	0910
	Light blue	I	800	159	1002
	Gold	I	725	305	0106
	Bright yellow	I	307	289	0104
	Light yellow	I	3078	292	0102
	Cream	I	739	1009	2014
	Purple	I	791	123	0904
	Dark mauve	I	553	99	0712
	Light mauve	I	554	96	0711
	Dark pink	I	892	28	0412
	Mid pink	I	3326	36	0606
	Light pink	I	818	271	0608
	Red	I	321	47	0510
	Dark red	I	815	43	0512
	Dark green	I	500	879	1705
	Mid green	I	368	214	1310
	Light green	I	369	1043	1309
	Dark grey green	I	502	876	1703
	Light grey green	I	504	1042	1701
	Dark olive green	I	3011	924	1607
	Light olive green	I	3013	854	1605

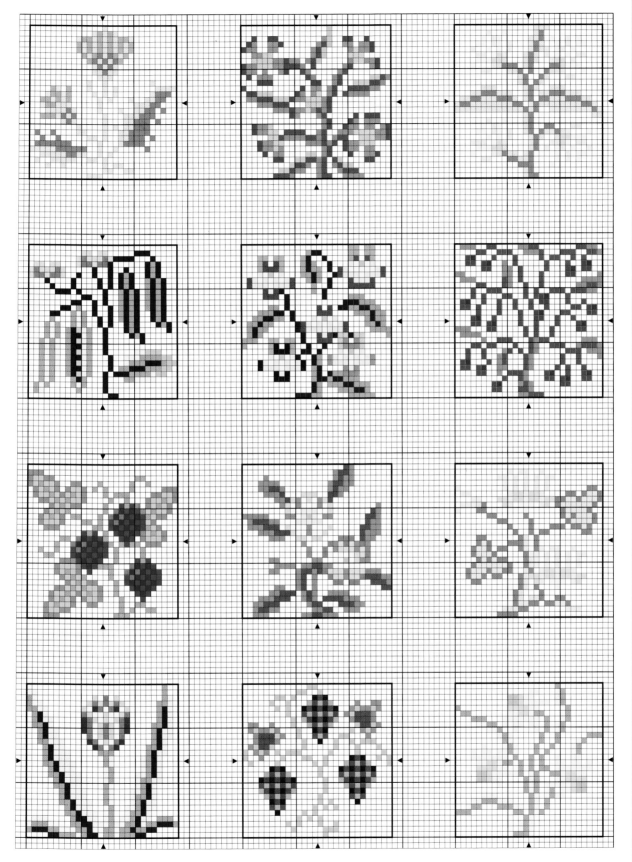

Fig 2.11 **Chart for the Slips bed**

Fig 2.12 **The Cotehele bed (shown with the Blackwork bedcover and pillow – see pages 42–3)**

Cotehele Bed Hangings

This project is shown as a half-tester bed (*see* Fig 2.12) a small canopy extending between one-third and one-half of the length of the bed. The canopy is supported by chains hanging from the ceiling and by the top of the bed.

The design is based on a crewelwork bed at Cotehele House, St Dominick, near Saltash, Cornwall. The original is worked in red worsted wool on a linen ground. Its scrolling stem motif is rather larger than usually seen, being approximately 23cm (9in) in diameter. The bed is dated about 1680.

Cotehele Bed Hangings

Materials

Evenweave linen or cotton (35 or 36 count)
    4 curtains: 110 x 30cm (43 x 12in)
    2 curtains: 80 x 30cm (32 x 12in)
1 skein stranded cotton in desired colour
Tapestry needle: No. 26
Tacking cotton
Sewing thread to match fabric or PVA fabric glue

Size

Each repeat: 68w x 60h stitches, 50 x 43mm (2 x 1⅝in)
As a border: 68w x 51h stitches, 50 x 35mm (2 x 1⅜in)
Individual items as per pattern

Working method

1 Make paper patterns for all the required pieces as directed on page 10. The curtains shown are hanging as flat panels and are one pattern repeat wide (*see* Fig 2.13). If you choose to have gathered curtains, one and a half pattern repeats are needed, 75mm (3in) wide, with turnings added.

2 Using the paper patterns, mark the fabric with tacking stitches to show the outlines of each piece. Leave sufficient fabric between pieces to allow for the turnings. Also mark with tacking stitches the vertical centres of each piece.

3 If all the above pieces have been marked out together on one piece of fabric, mount the whole piece into a rectangular stretcher frame, or place a ring frame on the area to be worked. If the pieces have been marked out separately, mount each one, as required in a card mount. This process is described in Materials and working methods (*see* page 136).

4 Refer to the chart (*see* Fig 2.15) and begin working either at the lower edge of a curtain or the centre of a valance. Use one strand of stranded cotton in the desired colour and back stitch throughout.

5 When the embroidery is complete, remove the fabric from the frame.

6 Check the measurements of the completed pieces against the bed as the upper valance is mounted outside the curtains and may need to be a little longer than expected.

7 Make up the hangings as shown on page 34.

Fig 2.13 **The bed curtain**

Fig 2.14 **The bed valance**

Cotehele Bed Hangings: suggested colours

		Skeins	DMC	Anchor	Madeira
	Dark red	1	816	1005	0512
	Dark blue	1	824	132	1010
	Dark green	1	319	683	1313

Fig 2.15 **Chart for the Cotehele bed**

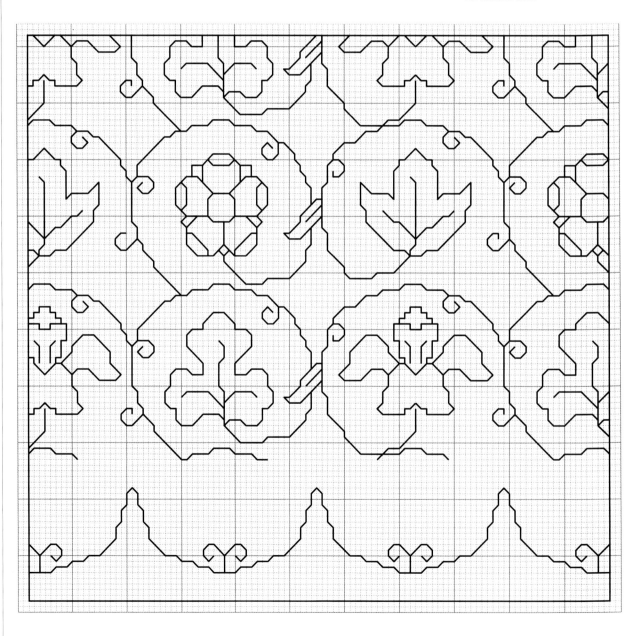

Fig 2.16 **The Crewelwork bed**

Crewelwork Bed Hangings

During the seventeenth century, the scrolling stem of the previous century developed into the 'tree of life' motif. As the century progressed, the design became heavier and more exotic with all manner of birds and animals added. This style coincided with the baroque period when a fashion for heavy, ornate sculptured decoration was used. With the eighteenth century, crewelwork designs became light, delicate and airy. This design can be used for a set of window curtains if desired, although window curtains were not common during the Tudor and Stuart periods.

See also instructions for Crewelwork bedcover (*see* page 47).

Crewelwork Bed Hangings

Materials
Lightweight pure silk or cotton:
  4 curtains: 110 x 30cm (43 x 12in)
  2 curtains: 80 x 30cm (32 x 12in)
Stranded cotton as listed on the colour key
Embroidery or crewel needle: No. 10
Tacking cotton
Sewing thread to match fabric or PVA fabric glue

Size
Curtains: 180 x 75mm (7 x 3in)
Valance: 25mm (1in) wide x required
  length
Individual items as per pattern

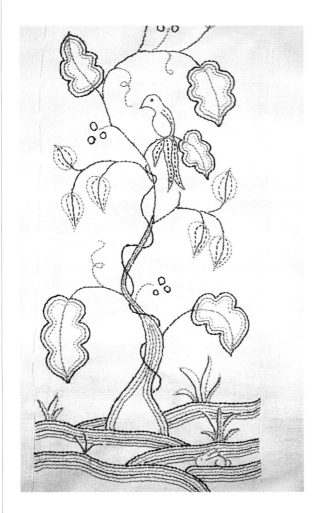

Fig 2.17 **The Crewelwork bed curtain**

Working method

A light-coloured fabric shows the embroidery to advantage. The original bed hangings would have been on a cream linen and cotton mix.

1 Make paper patterns for all the required items as directed (*see* Fig 2.2, page 11). The curtains will gather easily for this project.

2 Using the paper patterns, mark the fabric with tacking stitches to show the outlines of each piece. Leave sufficient fabric between the pieces to allow for the turnings.

3 Transfer the design (*see* Fig 2.18) to each item by either tracing through the fabric or ironing off a photocopy: these methods are

detailed in Methods of transferring designs (*see* page 142). Repeat the valance pattern to fit the length of the valance.

4 If all the pieces have been marked up together on one piece of fabric, mount the fabric into a rectangular stretcher frame, or place a ring frame on the area to be worked. If the pieces have been marked on separate pieces of fabric, mount each piece as required in a card mount. This process is described in Materials and working methods (*see* page 136).

5 Using one strand of stranded cotton, follow the lines of the design with a small back stitch, (*see* Figs 2.17 and 2.19). The colours and stitches on the valance are the same as shown for the curtains.

6 When the embroidery is complete, remove the fabric from the frame.

7 Check the measurements of the completed pieces against the bed as the upper valance is mounted outside the curtains and may need to be a little longer than expected.

8 Make the hangings up as shown on page 34.

Fig 2.18 **Patterns for the Crewelwork bed**

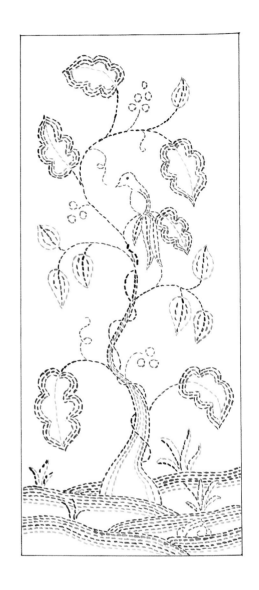

Fig 2.19 **Coloured stitch diagram for the Crewelwork bed**

Crewelwork Bed Hangings

		Skeins	DMC	Anchor	Madeira
	Dark green	I	500	879	1705
	Mid green	I	502	876	1703
	Light green	I	504	1042	1701
	Dark olive green	I	730	924	1614
	Light olive green	I	734	280	1610
	Dark brown	I	839	1050	1913
	Light brown	I	841	379	1911
	Gold	I	680	907	2210
	Dark red	I	902	897	0601
	Blue	I	798	137	0911

Fig 2.20 **The Fabric and Braid Trimmed bed in the style of the Melville bed in the Victoria and Albert Museum**

Fabric and Braid Trimmed Bed

During the seventeenth century the baroque style was in vogue with an emphasis on heavy, ornate gilded carving. This style was reflected in the rich beds of the time with much of the structure of the bed covered with silk fabric, which in turn was decorated with braids, fringes and tassels. A good example can be seen in the Victoria and Albert Museum in London: the Melville bed, a seventeenth-century half-tester, covered in white silk and trimmed with deep red braids, fringes and tassels.

It would be very difficult to cover an existing ready-made bed, so I suggest purchasing a kit or making one from scratch. The bed shown in Fig 2.20 is a half-tester, but a four-poster can be made in the same way.

Fabric and Braid Trimmed Bed

Materials

Lightweight silk or cotton fabric: 100 x 50cm (39 x 20in)

Braid, 2m (6ft 6in)

PVA fabric glue

PVA wood glue

Stripwood:

  3mm (⅛in) thick x desired bed width 75, 90 or 100mm
    (3, 3½ or 4in) x 450mm (18in) long

  6 x 6mm (¼ x ¼in) square x 750mm (30in) long

  12 x 3mm (½ x ⅛in) x 450mm (18in) long

  25 x 3mm (1 x ⅛in) x 450mm (18in) long

Miniature cornice moulding: 450mm (18in) long

Size

As desired

See also instructions for Braided Silk bedcover (see page 50).

29

Half-tester bed: working method

1 From stripwood 3mm (⅛in) thick x desired bed-width, cut one headpiece (A), 180mm (7in) long (*see* Fig 2.21).

2 Cut two posts (B) from 6mm (¼in)-square stripwood, 180mm (7in) high.

3 Cut one shaped headboard (C) from 3mm (⅛in)-thick stripwood. Cut the shape illustrated roughly with a craft knife and finish with a file or sandpaper.

4 Cut the fabric for the headpiece with a 25mm (1in) turning on all sides. Mark the pattern in position in the upper half (*see* Fig 2.22A) and decorate with braid, using either stitching or fabric glue. Glue the fabric to the headpiece by folding the edges to the back and gluing.

5 Cover the two posts with fabric using glue in the same way, with the raw edges to the back of the post.

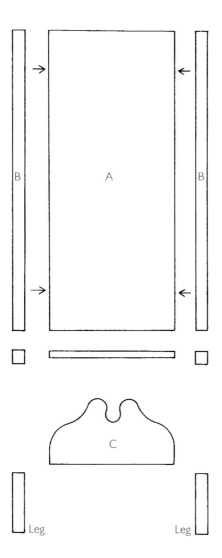

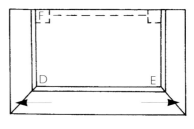

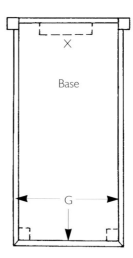

Fig 2.21 **Parts required to make a half-tester bed**

Fig 2.22A **Pattern for braid design**

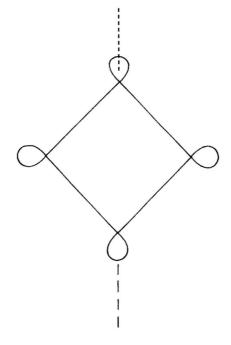

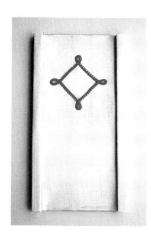

Fig 2.23 **The fabric-covered headpiece and posts when joined**

6 Glue the two posts to the headpiece ensuring that the tops and bottoms are level (*see* Fig 2.23).

7 Using a thin layer of PVA wood glue, cover the front and edges of the headboard. Allow to dry completely.

8 Cut a piece of fabric with 25mm (1in) turning for the headboard and, with a warm iron, press the fabric on to the front. Then snip into the turnings and, using the iron, turn the edges over and secure the excess turnings to the back with glue (*see* Fig 2.24).

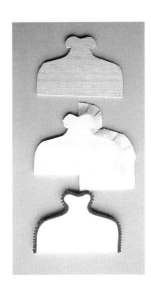

Fig 2.24 **Covering the headboard:**
Top: wooden shape with dry PVA glue
Centre: fabric applied, showing snipped turnings
Bottom: completed headboard trimmed with braid

Fig 2.22B **Pattern for valance border (see page 32)**

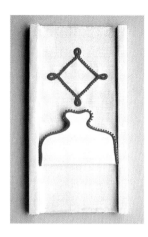

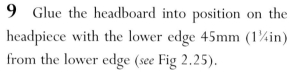

Fig 2.25 **Headpiece with headboard in place**

Fig 2.26 **Cornice covered with fabric**

9 Glue the headboard into position on the headpiece with the lower edge 45mm (1¾in) from the lower edge (*see* Fig 2.25).

10 Using 25 x 3mm (1 x ⅛in) stripwood, cut one piece to form the vertical front of the canopy, with a 45° mitre at each end. D–E (*see* Fig 2.21) should be the inside measurement of the mitred ends. Also cut two pieces 50mm (2in) with a mitre at one end only: F–D (*see* Fig 2.21).

11 Glue these pieces at the mitred corners to form the three sides of the canopy. Allow to dry.

12 Cover the inside and outside with a thin layer of PVA fabric glue and allow to dry.

13 Cut a strip of fabric 50mm (2in) wide, long enough to cover the three canopy sides. Using a warm iron, seal the fabric to the outside. Turn the remaining fabric to the inside and seal to the wood.

14 Cut three pieces of cornice moulding with mitred corners to fit around the outside of the canopy. Paint the pieces with fabric glue and allow to dry. To cover, seal a strip of fabric on to each piece with the toe of an iron (*see* Fig 2.26).

15 Glue the covered cornice pieces into position on the outside of the canopy (*see* Fig 2.27).

16 Glue the completed canopy into position at the top of the headpiece (*see* Fig 2.20).

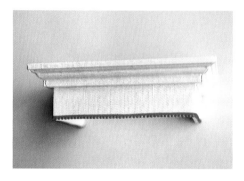

Fig 2.27 **Completed covered canopy for the half-tester**

17 Cut two pieces of 6mm (¼in)-square stripwood 41mm (1⅝in) for the two legs.

18 From the stripwood used for the headpiece, cut the base to the desired length of the bed, about 140–150mm (5½–6in).

19 Glue the two legs to the underside of the base at the end of the bed. Allow to dry.

20 Glue the base to the headpiece below the headboard. Reinforce underneath with a piece of 6mm (¼in)-square stripwood (X) Fig 2.21.

21 Using 12 x 3mm (½ x ⅛in) stripwood, cut three pieces, with mitred corners, to fit around the outside edge of the base (G) (*see* Fig 2.21).

22 Complete and fit the bed furnishings (*see* page 34) as directed later in this chapter; lower valance first (*see* Fig 2.22B), then curtains and bedcover (*see* pages 35 and 50).

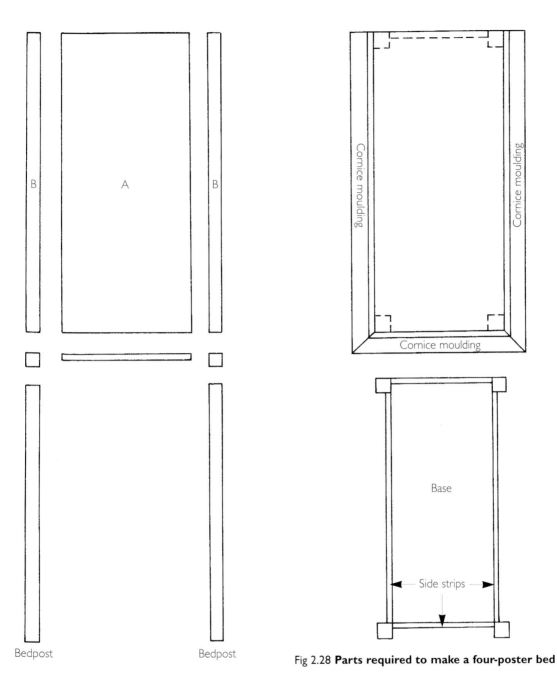

Bedpost   Bedpost

Fig 2.28 **Parts required to make a four-poster bed**

Four-poster bed: working method

1 Follow steps 1 to 9 as given for the half-tester (*see* Figs 2.22–2.25).

10 Cut two posts for the foot of the bed from 6mm (¼ in)-square stripwood, 180mm (7in) high and cover as before. You may prefer to purchase a pair of turned bedposts for this end of the bed, in which case, stain and varnish as required.

11 Cut a base as in step 18 for the half-tester.

12 Using the 12 x 3mm (½ in x ⅛ in) stripwood, cut three pieces to fit the two sides and the foot of the base.

33

13 Assemble by gluing the side strips to the base. Allow to dry. Glue the base, as before, to the headpiece and, keeping the base level, glue the bedposts into position. Allow to dry.

14 Now assemble the canopy by cutting three lengths of the 25 x 3mm (1 x ⅛in) stripwood, with mitred corners to fit vertically around the outer edge of the four bedposts. Cover with fabric as in steps 12 and 13 for the half-tester.

15 Glue into position level with the top edge of the headpiece and bedposts.

16 Cut and cover the cornice pieces, as for the half-tester, steps 14 and 15.

17 Glue the cornice pieces into position.

18 Complete and fit the bed furnishings as follows; lower valances first, then curtains and bedcover (*see* page 34–5 and 50).

Making up and fitting bed hangings

Lower valance

The lower valance is usually fitted first and may be in three separate sections or in one long strip, as in the Fabric and Braid Trimmed bed.

Separate sections

1 Cut out a piece of Bond-a-web, or similar bonding agent, to cover the reverse side of each valance section and iron on. Remove the paper backing.

2 Fold up the lower turning and press with the iron to secure.

3 Fold down the top turning and secure as above.

4 Check the length of each piece against the bed and turn under each end and secure with a little fabric glue.

5 Glue each piece into position on the sides of the bed base.

One long strip

1 Cut out a piece of Bond-a-web, or similar bonding agent, to cover the reverse side of the lower valance strip and iron on. Remove the paper backing.

2 Fold and secure the lower and top turnings as above.

3 Check the length against the bed, allowing for a pleat at each bottom corner.

4 Fold the valance to make the pleats (*see* Fig 2.20) and secure the top edges with a spot of fabric glue. Also turn and glue the ends under. Leave to dry.

5 Glue the lower valance to the edges of the bed base as above.

Headpiece and tester

1 Fold under the top and lower turnings and secure the fabric glue or stitching.

2 Fold under and secure the side turnings in the same way.

3 Glue the headpiece to the bed by the top edge.

4 Glue the tester inside the roof of the bed by all four sides.

Curtains

The first two projects have flat panels for curtains which are made up as follows:

1 Iron a piece of Bond-a-web or similar bonding agent to the reverse of the embroidered panels.

2 Trim the lower edge turning to 6mm (¼in), turn under and press with an iron.

3 Check the measurement required for the height of the curtain against the bed and turn under the top edge as for the lower.

4 Trim the turnings on each side to half the width of the curtain and press under as above. The turnings should then cover the reverse side of the embroidered panel.

5 Glue each panel inside the top canopy by the top edge.

Gathering method

The remaining projects have gathered curtains which are made as follows:

1 Trim the lower edge turning and either stitch a narrow hem, or secure with fabric glue used sparingly.

2 Trim and turn the side edges in the same way.

3 On the reverse side of the fabric, mark a grid of dots with a soluble fabric pen or dressmakers' carbon (*see* Fig 2.29).

4 Thread a needle with polyester sewing thread and fasten on with a double stitch. Pick up a tiny stitch at each dot working horizontally across the curtain. Leave the thread free at the end of each row (*see* Fig 2.30).

Fig 2.29 **The placement of dots in preparation for gathering**

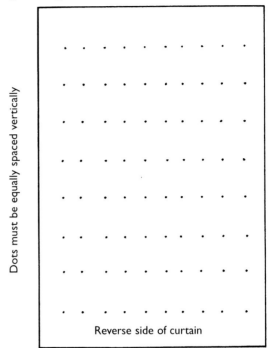

Dots must be equally spaced vertically

Reverse side of curtain

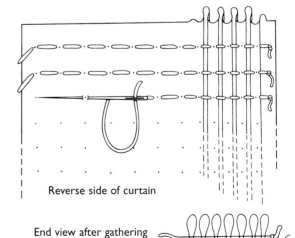

Reverse side of curtain

End view after gathering

Fig 2.30 **Gathering the curtain**

35

5 When all the gathering threads are in place, draw up each row and fasten off the threads. As each row is gathered, stroke a needle down each pleat so that it hangs correctly.

6 When all the rows are gathered and fastened off, hold the fabric in front of a steam iron and allow the steam to penetrate the pleats. Take care to protect your fingers.

7 Leave the fabric gathered until completely dry.

8 Gently unfasten and remove the gathering threads.

Using a commercial pleater

1 Turn and secure any hems and side seams as in steps 1 and 2 above.

2 Dampen the fabric slightly and lay it on the pleater with the slots running vertically down the curtain. Using one of the cards provided, push the fabric into the first slot.

3 Leaving the first card in place, push the fabric into the next slot with the second card (*see* Fig 2.31).

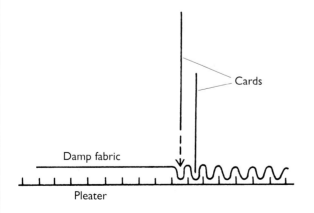

Fig 2.31 **Using a commercial pleater**

5 Continue, using the two cards, to pleat the fabric, always holding a card in the previous pleat.

6 When the whole curtain has been pleated, hold a steam iron over it without actually touching the pleater.

7 Bond a narrow strip of Bond-a-web to the top edge of the curtain and leave to dry completely.

8 Gently ease the curtain out of the pleater.

Attach each curtain to the inside top rails or canopy of the bed with a little fabric glue.

Upper valance

1 Follow steps 1 to 4 of the directions given for a lower valance in separate sections.

2 Using glue sparingly, secure the upper valance to the outside of the top rails of a four-poster bed, or to the inside of the canopy on a half-tester.

Window curtains

During the timescale outlined in this book, curtains were not generally hung at windows. Early houses had shutters or, at most, a cloth hung across the lower part of the window opening. Many grand houses also had folding window shutters. However, if you wish to make curtains for your house, the method described above for bed curtains can be used. A greater variety of curtain styles are shown in the companion volumes for Georgian and Victorian dolls' houses.

3 Bedcovers and pillows

In Tudor and Stuart times, a bedcover would not necessarily match a set of bed hangings. The first three projects in this chapter could be mixed and matched with any of the bed hangings in Chapter 2. However, the crewelwork and braided bedcovers (*see* pages 47 and 50) would probably be most suited to the beds on which they are shown in Figs 2.16 and 2.20.

The bedcover in the sixteenth and seventeenth centuries rarely hung to the floor, covering the lower valance. More commonly, it would hang down to cover only the top of the lower valance. On a miniature bedcover for a four-poster bed it is sometimes advisable to remove the two corners at the foot of the bed in order to reduce the bulk, depending on the thickness of the chosen fabric. All the designs can be altered by simply omitting the corners.

The first project, Scrolling Stem bedcover and pillow (Fig 3.2), is based on the dominant scrolling stem design, presented here in a counted thread technique. The stem divides the ground into compartments. Flower motifs were then placed into each area.

The second project, Blackwork bedcover and pillow (Fig 3.5), shows another popular choice of the period. Many household and costume items were worked in blackwork; although not always in black, sometimes in red or blue. There were three main types of blackwork technique; shapes filled with counted patterns; speckling, which imitated the woodblock prints and was worked in seeding stitches; and Holbein stitch, a reversible double running stitch used on collars, cuffs and where both sides of the fabric would be seen.

The third project, Gold Trellis bedcover and pillow (Fig 3.8), shows another form, where the compartments containing the flower motifs are divided by a trellis rather than the scrolling stem.

The Crewelwork bedcover (Fig 3.12) reflects a design form dominant in the seventeenth century, based on the 'tree of life' motif, a highly ornate tree growing from a mound.

The final project, Braided Silk bedcover (Fig 3.15), is of plain fabric with a decoration of applied braids and tassels. This was mostly used in the seventeenth century when rich, exotic fabrics were more available, although some examples from very wealthy houses date from the previous century.

Matching pillows have been included as these would have been used during the day when visitors were being received in the bed chamber.

Making a pattern for a bedcover or pillow

1 Measure the width of the bed, A–B. Measure the length and subtract 15mm (½ in), A–C in Fig 3.1.

2 Extend the three sides to the desired drop, D–E.

3 Add 10mm (⅜ in) turning to all four sides.

4 If required, remove the two corners at the lower edge.

5 A bolster pillow will be the width of the bed, as A–B above, by 30mm (1¼ in), F–G.

6 A pillow will be half the width, A–B divided by two, and 30mm (1¼ in), F–G as above.

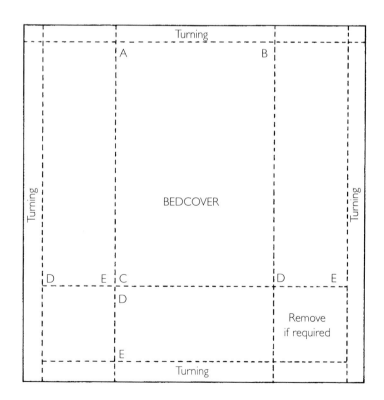

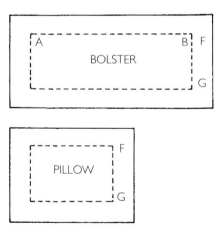

Fig 3.1 **Making patterns for bedcovers, bolsters and pillows**

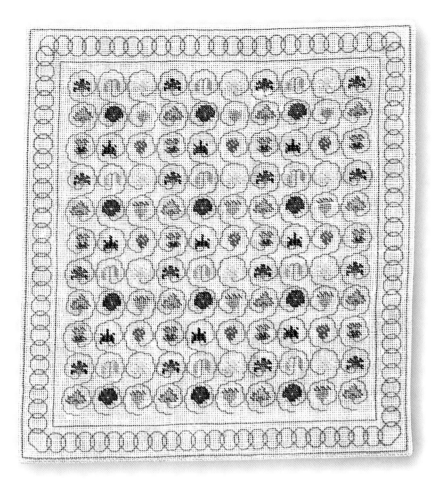

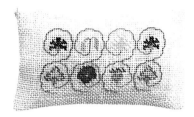

Fig 3.2 **The Scrolling Stem bedcover and pillow**

Scrolling Stem Bedcover and Pillow

The scrolling stems on this bedcover enclose some of the popular motifs of the sixteenth century, including the rose, honeysuckle, pansy, columbine and pea pod, Figs 3.2 and 3.3. It is presented here as a counted thread project although an original would have been worked in surface stitchery.

This bedcover may be used with the Oxburgh bed hangings (*see* page 13).

Scrolling Stem Bedcover and Pillow

Materials

Evenweave linen (35 count): 200mm (8in) square

Lightweight silk lining: 200mm (8in) square

Evenweave linen (35 count): 100mm (4in) square

Lightweight silk lining: 100mm (4in) square

Stranded cottons as listed in colour key

Sewing thread to match fabric

Tapestry needle: No. 24 or 26

Size

Pattern repeat: 44 x 45 stitches

Border: 15 stitches wide

153 x 142mm (6 x 5⅝in)

Working method for bedcover

1 Mark the outside edges, and the vertical and horizontal centres with tacking stitches.

2 Mount the fabric into a small rectangular frame: *see* page 137.

3 Refer to the chart, Fig 3.4, and begin with the border at one of the lower corners. Use one strand of stranded cotton throughout and back stitch where the chart shows a line, or tent stitch where there is a solid square on the chart.

4 When a corner and part of two sides have been worked, it is easier to place the central design by counting from the border. When the embroidery is complete, remove the fabric from the frame.

5 Make up as described on page 51.

Working method for pillow

1 Mark the edges with tacking stitches and mount in a small rectangular frame: *see* page 137.

2 Refer to the chart, Fig 3.4, and work an area of the central pattern in the centre of the pillow. The exact number of motifs will depend on the size of the pillow.

3 When the embroidery is complete, remove the fabric from the frame.

4 Make up as described on page 51.

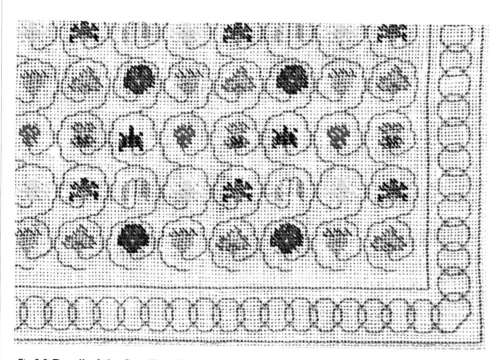

Fig 3.3 **Detail of the Scrolling Stem pattern**

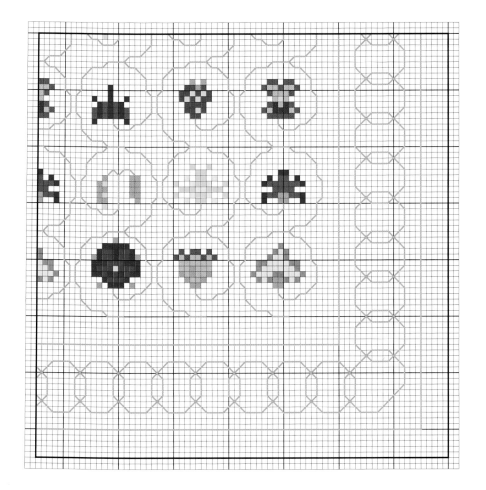

Fig 3.4 **Chart for Scrolling Stem bedcover**

Scrolling Stem Bedcover and Pillow

		Skeins	DMC	Anchor	Madeira
	Green	1	470	266	1410
	Dark pink	1	602	63	0702
	Light pink	1	3326	36	0606
	Dark mauve	1	553	99	0712
	Light mauve	1	554	96	0711
	Dark red	1	816	1005	0512
	Light red	1	321	47	0510
	Dark blue	1	820	134	0904
	Light blue	1	798	137	0911
	Yellow	1	743	305	0113

Blackwork Bedcover and Pillow

The motifs for this bedcover and pillow are based on patterns used for household items during the late sixteenth and early seventeenth centuries. This bedcover can be used with the Cotehele bed hangings (*see* page 22).

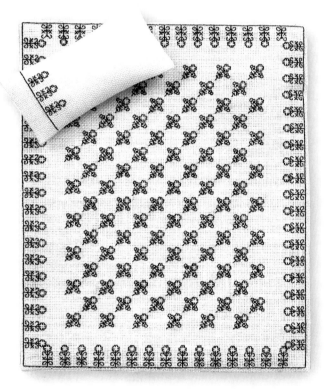

Working method for bedcover

1 Mark the outside edges, and the vertical and horizontal centres with tacking stitches.

2 Mount the fabric into a small rectangular frame: *see* page 137.

3 Refer to the chart, Fig 3.6, and begin the border at one of the lower corners. Use one strand of stranded cotton and back stitch throughout. When a corner and part of two sides have been worked it is easier to position the central motifs.

4 When the embroidery is complete, remove the fabric from the frame.

5 Make up as described on page 51.

Fig 3.5 **Blackwork bedcover and pillow**

Blackwork Bedcover and Pillow

Materials

Evenweave linen (35 count): 200mm (8in) square

Lightweight silk lining: 200mm (8in) square

Evenweave linen (35 count): 100mm (4in) square

Lightweight silk lining: 100 (4in) square

Black stranded cotton or machine embroidery thread

Sewing thread to match fabric

Tapestry needle: No. 24 or 26

Size

Pattern repeat: 20 stitches square

Border: 13 stitches wide

155 x 127mm (6⅛ x 5in)

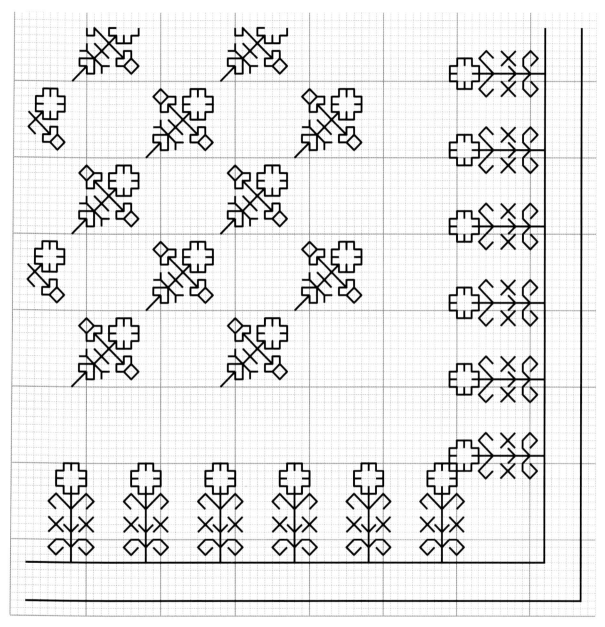

Fig 3.6 **Chart for Blackwork bedcover and pillow**

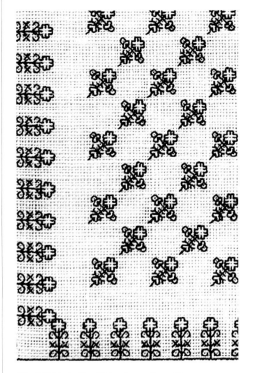

Fig 3.7 **Detail of blackwork pattern**

Working method for pillow

1 Mark the edges with tacking stitches and mount in a small rectangular frame or card mount: *see* page 137.

2 Refer to the chart, Fig 3.6, and work a section of the border pattern along one end of the pillow. Alternatively, two or three of the central motifs could be positioned in the centre of the pillow or on a bolster.

3 When the embroidery is complete, remove the fabric from the frame.

4 Make up as described on page 51.

Gold Trellis Bedcover and Pillow

A laid-work trellis divides the bedcover to accommodate a variety of flower motifs which were popular throughout the sixteenth and seventeenth centuries. The trellis is laid with a metallic gold thread to give a rich surface. A pillow can be worked using a section of the bedcover design. This bedcover looks good with the Slips bed hangings (*see* page 17).

Fig 3.8 **Gold Trellis bedcover**

44

Gold Trellis Bedcover and Pillow

Materials

Lightweight cotton, silk or crêpe de Chine: 200mm (8in) square

Lightweight silk lining: 200mm (8in) square

Lightweight cotton, silk or crêpe de Chine: 100mm (4in) square

Lightweight silk lining: 100mm (4in) square

Selection of stranded cottons: blues, pinks, mauves, greens, orange and red

Stranded metallic gold thread

Gold-coloured sewing thread

Sewing thread to match fabric

Embroidery needle: No. 10

Size

150mm (6in) square

Working method for bedcover

1 Take a photocopy of the trellis pattern, Fig 3.10, and iron it off on to the fabric, making sure the grain is straight.

2 Using two strands of the metallic thread, lay the trellis over the pattern lines. Stitch the trellis down with the gold-coloured sewing thread. The method for this is given in the Stitch Glossary on page 155 under laid work.

3 Work a flower motif in each compartment using one strand of stranded cotton and your colours freely as desired. Refer to Fig 3.11 for the options. The stitches used are, straight, detached chain and French knots (*see* Stitch Glossary, page 151).

4 Before working the line around the edge of the cover, make up as described on page 51.

5 Finally, work the outside line in stranded cotton using back stitch. This will keep the edge of your bedcover flat.

Working method for pillow

1 Either make a plain pillow to use with this cover, or transfer a section of the design to the required size. Embroider as for the cover and make up as directed on page 51.

Fig 3.9 **Detail of Gold Trellis bedcover**

45

Fig 3.10 **Pattern for the Gold Trellis bedcover**

Fig 3.11 **Stitches used in Gold Trellis bedcover**

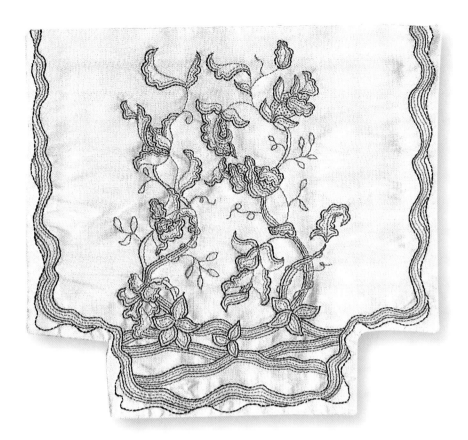

Fig 3.12 **Crewelwork bedcover**

Crewelwork Bedcover

The design for the crewelwork bedcover is typical of the seventeenth century and is designed to be used with Crewelwork bed hangings (*see* page 25). The leaves are based on a wall hanging, from about 1700, which is in the collection of the Embroiderers' Guild. You can make a pillow of plain fabric to use with this bedcover.

Working method

1 Transfer the design, Fig 3.13, on to one of the pieces of fabric, either with a fabric transfer pencil or by photocopy. Remember the latter will reverse the design (*see* page 143 for detailed instructions).

Crewelwork Bedcover

Materials

2 pieces lightweight silk or cotton: each 250mm (10in) square
Stranded cotton as listed in colour key
Embroidery needle: No. 10

Size

160 x 150mm (6¼ x 6in)

2 Mount the fabric into a rectangular frame (*see* page 137).

3 Refer to the coloured stitch diagram, Fig 3.14, and, using one strand of stranded cotton, work the design using back stitch. The red speckling within some of the leaves is worked with seeding stitches. *Do not work the outside*

47

Fig 3.13 **Pattern for Crewelwork bedcover**

wavy line of the design at this stage as this is worked
after the lining has been attached.

4 When the embroidery is complete, remove the fabric from the frame.

5 Press with an iron from the wrong side if necessary.

6 Trim the outside turnings to about 6mm (¼in) and turn under.

7 Prepare the lining, the second piece of fabric, in the same way and place the two pieces reverse sides together, Fig 3.16.

8 Stitch the two pieces together with sewing cotton.

9 Now work the outside wavy line of back stitch through both layers to give a flat finish to the edge.

Crewelwork Bedcover

		Skeins	DMC	Anchor	Madeira
	Dark green	1	319	683	1313
	Mid green	1	470	266	1410
	Light green	1	472	264	1414
	Dark gold	1	832	907	2202
	Light gold	1	834	874	2206
	Dark brown	1	839	1050	1913
	Light brown	1	841	378	1911
	Red	1	321	47	0510

Fig 3.14 **Coloured stitch diagram for the Crewelwork bedcover**

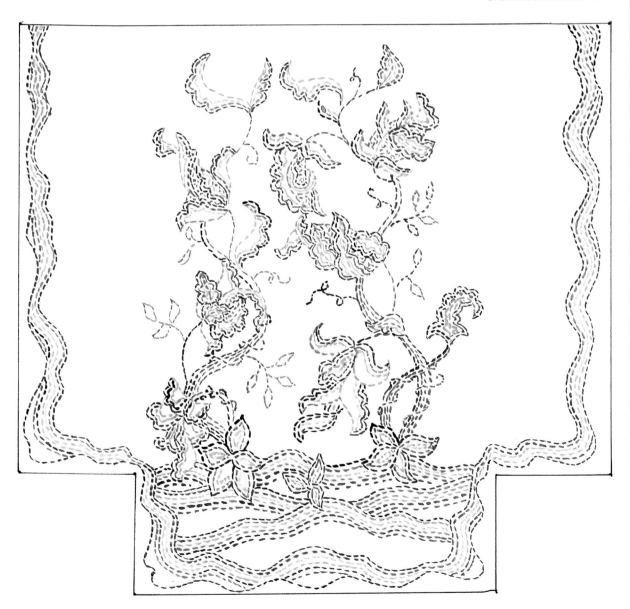

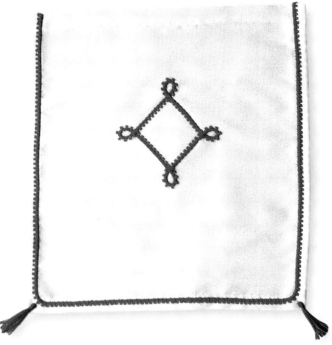

Fig 3.15 **Braided Silk bedcover**

Braided Silk Bedcover

Designed to be used with a Fabric and Braid Trimmed Bed (*see* page 29), this cover is very simple. You can make a plain pillow to use with it.

Working method

1 Cut two pieces of fabric to the desired size, adding on turnings.

2 Transfer the design on to one piece of fabric, *see* Fig 2.22. Place the fabric over the design and trace through with a fabric pen or pencil. The scalloped edging can be used if desired.

3 Stitch the braid on to the design.

4 Turn the edges of both pieces of fabric under, to the finished size, and stitch the edges together (*see* Fig 3.16).

5 Stitch a row of braid along the sides and lower edge through both layers of fabric.

6 Make and attach tassels (*see* page 147).

Braided Silk Bedcover

Materials

2 pieces lightweight silk or cotton fabric: each 250mm (10in) square

1m (39in) braid

Stranded cotton or machine embroidery thread for tassels

Sewing threads to match fabric and braid

Embroidery needle: No. 10

Size

As desired

Making up bedcovers, bolsters and pillows

Bedcovers

1 Fold under the outside turnings (*see* Fig 3.16) and place the front and back wrong sides together. If the corners have been cut away, reinforce with a small piece of iron-on interlining on the reverse before cutting into the corner turning.

2 Hem stitch the edges together with matching sewing thread.

3 Work any remaining embroidery through the edges of both fabrics, as directed in the individual projects.

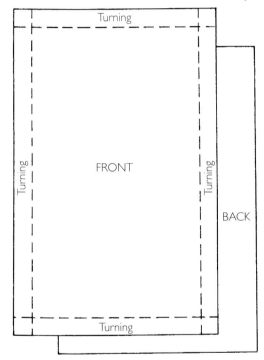

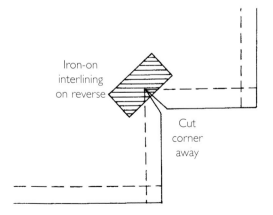

Fig 3.16 Making up a bedcover

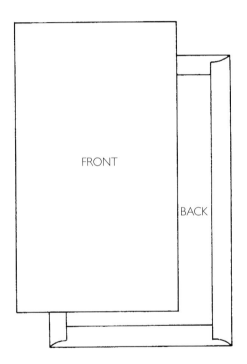

Bolsters and pillows

1 Cut two pieces the same size for the front and back.

2 Turn the two long sides and one end under on both pieces and place together as for the bedcover.

3 Stitch the three sides together.

4 Fill the bolster or pillow with either wadding, for a firm finish, or with small plastic beads if you want a softer look.

5 Stitch up the remaining side.

4 Cushions

Cushions were very important household items during the Tudor period as upholstered furniture was extremely rare. Therefore, stools, chairs and window seats required cushions of all shapes and sizes. In addition, there were smaller cushions for holding jewellery, for protecting the decorated covers of books and, very importantly, for use as pin cushions. Costume during the sixteenth and seventeenth century was largely pinned together – the petticoat, skirt, stomacher and sleeves being separate elements – making the pin cushion an essential item. Cushions remained numerous during the seventeenth century although upholstered furniture was, by then, more common.

Fig 4.1 **A variety of cushions in the Tudor and Stuart styles**

The same variety of dominant design features of the period are to be seen on surviving cushions: the scrolling stem, the tree of life, pictorial scenes, flowers, fruit, heraldic devices and Florentine patterns. The techniques used included blackwork, crewelwork, metal thread work, raised embroidery and canvaswork which was the most commonly used due to its durability.

Some of the cushions in this chapter, which are based on canvaswork originals, have been worked on evenweave linen to allow for greater detail. If the finished piece distorts, it will need to be blocked back into shape. This process is described on page 149.

Fig 4.2 **Oxburgh cushions**

Oxburgh Cushions

For details of the original designs, see page 12. A selection of cushions can be made using the charts given for the Oxburgh bed hangings (*see* pages 15–16).

Working method

Coloured evenweave has been used for the examples shown (*see* Figs 4.2, 4.3 and 4.4).

A natural colour could be used, or you can colour white fabric (as directed on page 145), which should be done first.

1 Cut the fabric into two pieces, each 100mm (4in) square to make one cushion front and one back.

2 Mount the cushion front into a card mount: *see* page 139.

3 Mark the vertical and horizontal centres with tacking stitches.

Oxburgh Cushions

Materials
For each cushion

Evenweave linen (32 or 35 count): 200 x 100mm (8 x 4in)

Stranded cotton as listed in colour key

Tacking cotton

Sewing thread to match fabric

Tapestry needle: No. 26

Small quantity of wadding or small beads

Size
When using 35-count fabric:

Square panel: 48 stitches square, 37mm (1⁷⁄₁₆ in) square

Octagonal panels: 40 x 40 stitches, 30 x 30mm (1³⁄₁₆ x 1³⁄₁₆ in)

Cruciform panels: 32 x 32 stitches, 25 x 25mm (1 x 1in)

A 32-count fabric will give a slightly larger cushion

4 Referring to the desired chart, begin near the centre, using one strand of stranded cotton and tent stitch throughout. It is easiest to work the main motifs first and then the colours that fill the background areas.

5 When the embroidery is complete, remove the fabric from the card mount.

6 Block into shape if necessary (*see* page 149).

7 Make up and fill the cushion as directed on page 66.

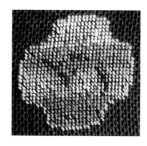

Fig 4.3 **Detail of the camel motif**

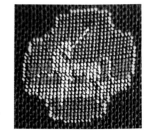

Fig 4.4 **Detail of the unicorn motif**

Fig 4.5 **Slips cushions**

Slips Cushions

For details of the background to use for these motifs, see page 18.

Using the chart for the Slips bed hangings, (*see* Fig 2.11, page 21), select the required motif.

A square cushion will require one motif in the centre and a rectangular or window-seat cushion will need two motifs placed side by side.

Slips Cushions

Materials
For each cushion
Same as those given for the Oxburgh cushions above

Size
As desired

Working method
As for Oxburgh cushions above.

Fig 4.6 **Huntsmen cushion**

Huntsmen Cushion

This design is based on a cushion made in about 1600, now found in the Victoria and Albert Museum, London. The original was made from canvaswork slips applied to a cream satin fabric. The applied motifs show cherry, pear and apple trees with flowers and two huntsmen. As these would have been selected from the books and herbals of the time, no regard has been given to the relative sizes of the chosen motifs.

Working method

1 Cut the fabric into two pieces each 100mm (4in) square for front and back of the cushion.
2 Mark front of the cushion with the outside edges, vertical and horizontal centres with tacking stitches and mount the fabric into a small frame or card mount (*see* page 139).
3 Refer to the chart (*see* Fig 4.8) and begin by working the centre tree. Use one strand of stranded cotton and tent stitch throughout.
4 Having worked the centre tree, the two huntsmen are easy to place, followed by the

Huntsmen Cushion

Materials
Evenweave linen (35 count): 200 x 100mm (8 x 4in)
Stranded cotton as listed in colour key
Tacking cotton
Sewing thread to match fabric
Tapestry needle: No. 26
Small quantity of wadding or small beads

Size
105 x 52 stitches, 77 x 37mm (3 x 1½in)

floral motifs and remaining trees.

5 When the embroidery is complete, remove the fabric from the frame or mount.

6 Block into shape if necessary (*see* page 149).

7 Make up and fill the cushion as directed on page 66.

Fig 4.7 **Huntsmen design**

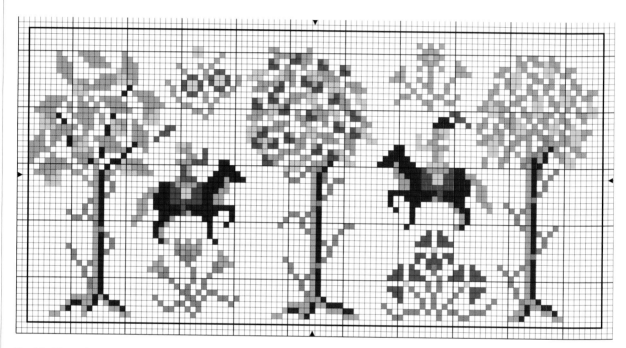

Fig 4.8 **Chart for Huntsmen cushion**

Huntsmen Cushion

		Skeins	DMC	Anchor	Madeira
	Dark green	I	470	266	1410
	Light green	I	472	264	1414
	Dark grey green	I	502	876	1703
	Gold	I	725	305	0106
	Dark brown	I	839	1050	1913
	Light brown	I	841	378	1911
	Red	I	321	47	0510
	Pink	I	352	9	0303
	Blue	I	798	137	0911

Heraldic Cushion

Cushions showing an heraldic device were very popular with families entitled to display arms. The design shown here is based on a canvaswork cushion in London's Victoria and Albert Museum, dated to the middle of the sixteenth century. The original shows the arms of the Warneford and Yates families set against a ground of foliage and small animals.

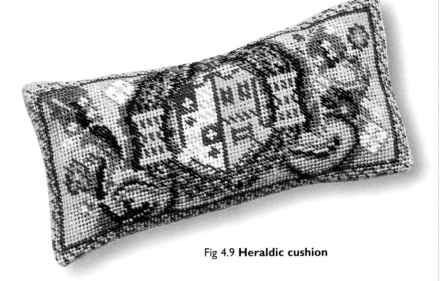

Fig 4.9 **Heraldic cushion**

Working method

1 As for Huntsmen Cushion (*see* page 55).

2 As for Huntsmen Cushion.

3 Refer to the chart (*see* Fig 4.10), and beginning with the coat of arms, work with one strand of stranded cotton using tent stitch throughout.

4 When the embroidery is complete, remove the fabric from the frame or mount.

5 Block into shape if necessary (*see* page 149).

6 Make up and fill the cushion as directed on page 66.

Heraldic Cushion

Materials

Evenweave linen (35 count): 200 x 100mm (8 x 4in)

Stranded cottons as listed in colour key

Tacking cotton

Sewing thread to match fabric

Tapestry needle: No. 26

Small quantity of wadding or small beads

Size

Each cushion

105 x 52 stitches, 77 x 37mm

(3 x 1½in)

Heraldic Cushion

		Skeins	DMC	Anchor	Madeira
	Dark red	I	815	43	0512
	Pink	I	352	9	0303
	Gold	I	725	305	0106
	Blue	I	799	145	0910
	Dark green	I	500	879	1705
	Mid green	I	502	876	1703
	Light green	I	504	1042	1701
	White	I	Blanc	White	White

Fig 4.10 **Chart for Heraldic cushion**

Fig 4.11 **Heraldic cushion design**

Intertwined Hearts Cushion

The simple design of intertwined hearts used for this design has been taken from a beautiful red satin cushion, c. 1600, in the Victoria and Albert Museum. The original is worked in gilt thread on a red background, with various flower motifs within the hearts. A blackwork cushion later in this chapter (*see* page 62) is also based on the same original, but being worked on a finer linen, greater detail can be achieved.

Fig 4.12 **Intertwined Hearts cushion**

Working method

1 Mark the outside edges and centres of the cushion with tacking stitches and mount the canvas into a small rectangular frame (*see* page 137).

2 Using tent stitch throughout, work the hearts with three strands of metallic thread.

3 Complete the background in your chosen colour using three strands of stranded cotton.

4 When the embroidery is complete, remove the fabric from the frame.

5 Block into shape if necessary (*see* page 149).

6 Make up as instructed using the lightweight fabric square for the back of the cushion, and fill as directed on page 67.

Intertwined Hearts Cushion

Materials

Single thread (mono) canvas (22 count): 100mm (4in) square

Lightweight silk or cotton fabric for cushion back: 100mm (4in) square

Stranded cotton as listed in colour key

Stranded gold metallic thread

Sewing thread to match fabric

Tapestry needle: No. 24 or 26

Small quantity of wadding or small beads

Size

33 x 34 stitches, 38mm (1½in) square

Intertwined Hearts Cushion

		Skeins	DMC	Anchor	Madeira
	Red	1	321	47	0510
Alternative colours					
	Blue	1	799	145	0910
	Green	1	500	879	1705
	Black	1	310	Black	Black

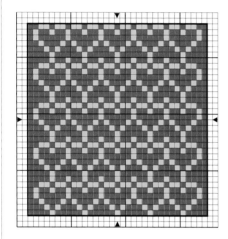

Fig 4.13 **Chart for Intertwined Hearts cushion**

Rose Trellis Cushion

This cushion represents a style of the late sixteenth and early seventeenth centuries. The roses are placed on a trellis with slip motifs within the spaces. Many cushions in this style survive, some with lilies or other popular flowers of the time.

Fig 4.14 **Rose Trellis cushion**

Rose Trellis Cushion

Materials

Single thread (mono) canvas (22 count): 100mm (4in) square

Lightweight silk or cotton fabric for cushion back: 100mm (4in) square

Stranded cotton as listed in colour key

Sewing thread to match fabric

Tapestry needle: No. 24 or 26

Small quantity of wadding or small beads

Size

33 stitches square, 38mm (1½in) square

Working method

1 Mark the outside edges and centres of the cushion with tacking stitches and mount the canvas into a small rectangular frame (*see* page 137).

2 Using tent stitch throughout, work the design, beginning with the main roses and trellis, using three strands of stranded cotton.

3 Fill in the background colour.

4 When the embroidery is complete, remove the fabric from the frame.

5 Block into shape if necessary (*see* page 149).

6 Make up as instructed using the lightweight fabric square for the back of the cushion, and fill as directed on page 67.

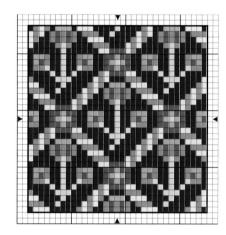

Fig 4.15 **Chart for Rose Trellis cushion**

Rose Trellis Cushion

		Skeins	DMC	Anchor	Madeira
	Red	1	321	47	0510
	Pink	1	352	9	0303
	Gold	1	725	305	0106
	Dark green	1	500	879	1705
	Mid green	1	502	876	1703
	Light green	1	504	1042	1701

Blackwork Cushions

Blackwork was a very popular choice of technique during the sixteenth and seventeenth centuries. Three main types were used: patterned fillings, speckling and Holbein (double running) stitch where the piece needed to be reversible.

The floral hearts design (*see* Figs 4.17 and 4.19) is based on an original cushion dated c. 1600. The interlocking hearts contain a suggestion of tiny floral motifs. Shown here as a square cushion, the chart can be used for any shape required or used as an all-over pattern on any item.

The second cushion design (*see* Figs 4.18 and 4.20) with a single flower motif within a border, is taken from a sampler from the early seventeenth century.

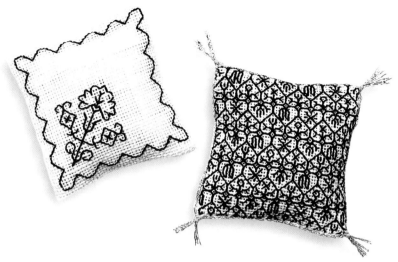

Fig 4.16 **Blackwork cushions**

Working method for both cushions

1 Cut the fabric into two pieces, each 100mm (4in) square.

2 On one piece of fabric, mark the outside edges and centres of the cushion with tacking stitches and mount the fabric into a small rectangular frame (*see* page 137).

Blackwork Cushions

Materials

For each cushion

Evenweave linen (35 count): 200 x 100mm (8 x 4in)

Black sewing or machine embroidery cotton

Sewing thread to match fabric

Tapestry needle: No. 26

Small quantity of wadding or small beads

Size

Both designs: 48 stitches square, 36mm (1⅜in) square

3 Refer to the relevant chart and work the pattern using the sewing or machine embroidery cotton and backstitch throughout.

4 Begin the floral hearts pattern in the middle of the lower edge and the single flower design from one corner.

5 When the embroidery is complete, remove the fabric from the frame.

6 Make up and fill the cushions as directed on page 66.

Fig 4.17 **Floral hearts design**

Fig 4.18 **Single flower motif**

Fig 4.19 **Chart for floral hearts cushion**

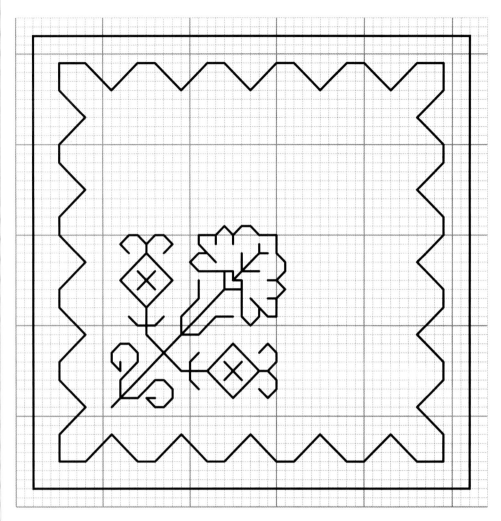

Fig 4.20 **Chart for single flower cushion**

Crewelwork Cushions

The designs for these cushions are based on a four-poster bed in the Victoria and Albert Museum in London. The bed was worked by Abigail Pett in wool on a linen and cotton fabric and is signed and dated: A.B. 1675. The designs are rather naive with individual motifs of plant forms, small scenes and animals.

Working method

1 Cut the fabric into two halves, each 100mm (4in) square.

2 Refer to the patterns (*see* Fig 4.22) and transfer the desired design on to one piece of fabric. Either trace with a fabric pencil or pen, or transfer a photocopy (*see* page 143). Mount the fabric into a small frame (*see* page 137).

3 Referring to the stitch diagram (*see* Fig 4.23) place the colours and stitches

Fig 4.21 **Crewelwork cushions**

as indicated. Use one strand of stranded cotton and backstitch, with seeding stitches on the bird (Design 2) and on the large leaf of Design 3.

4 When the embroidery is complete, remove the fabric from the frame.

5 Make up and fill the cushions as directed on page 66.

Fig 4.22 **Patterns for Crewelwork cushions. Left to right: Design 1, Design 2, Design 3**

Crewelwork Cushions

Materials

For each cushion

Lightweight silk or cotton fabric: 200 x 100mm (8 x 4in)

Stranded cottons as listed in colour key

Sewing cotton to match fabric

Embroidery needle: No. 10

Small amount of wadding or small beads

Size

38mm (1½in) square, or as desired

65

Crewelwork Cushions

		Skeins	DMC	Anchor	Madeira
	Dark green	1	500	879	1705
	Mid green	1	502	876	1703
	Light green	1	504	1042	1701
	Dark brown	1	839	1050	1913
	Light brown	1	841	378	1911
	Gold	1	725	305	0106

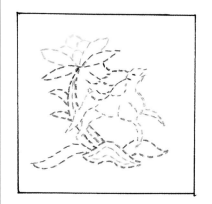  

Fig 4.23 **Coloured stitch diagrams for Crewelwork cushions. From left to right: Design 1, Design 2, Design 3**

Fig 4.24 **Close-up details of Crewelwork cushions**

Making up cushions

1 Trim the seam allowances on the front and back of the cushion to about 6mm (¼in) (*see* Fig 4.25A).

2 Fold the edges under to the reverse side (*see* Fig 4.25B) and stitch the front and back of the cushion together, leaving part of one side open.

3 Fill the cushion, *see* below, and complete the stitching to close the opening.

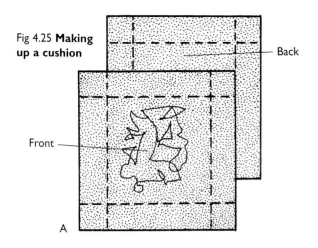

Fig 4.25 **Making up a cushion**

Back

Front

A

Back

Front

B

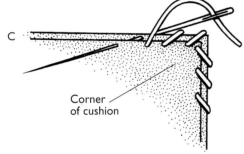

C

Corner
of cushion

Filling cushions

To obtain a firmly padded effect, fill the cushion with wadding or kapok. Pull the filling into very small pieces and fill the corners first. Do not overfill the cushion.

For a softer look, fill the cushion with small plastic or glass beads. When the opening has been stitched up the cushion can be pushed into a corner of a chair, leaving a realistic dent.

Alternative edgings for cushions

The most simple edging is achieved by using an oversewing stitch when sewing up the cushion edges (*see* Fig 4.26A). A contrasting thread can be used if desired. Alternatively, a couched thread can be laid to give a corded edge (*see* Fig 4.26B). When using the couched method, a simple 'tassel' can be made at each corner by leaving a loop of thread. The loop can then be cut and trimmed to simulate a tassel (*see* Fig 4.26C).

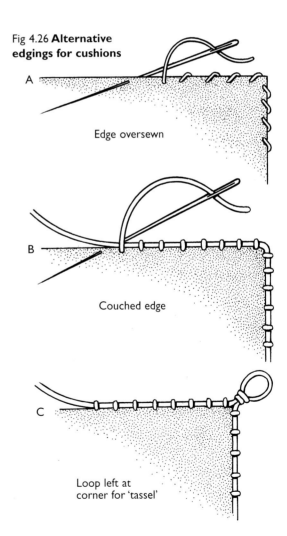

Fig 4.26 **Alternative edgings for cushions**

A

Edge oversewn

B

Couched edge

C

Loop left at corner for 'tassel'

5 Chair covers and footstools

Upholstered chairs, settees and footstools became more common during the seventeenth century. Cushions of all sizes and shapes were used prior to this. The designs used reflected the popular trends of the times: the tree of life form, Florentine patterns and scrolling stems dividing the ground into compartments that were filled with flower motifs.

The charted designs in this chapter can be used to cover ready-made or kit forms of chairs, settees and footstools. Alternatively, items can be made using plans or instructions from the many books on miniature furniture making. The embroidery designs mainly consist of all-over patterns which can be worked to the required size and shape needed.

Canvaswork Patterns

The three designs shown in Fig 5.1 can be worked within any size or shape required.

If using a ready-made chair, make a paper pattern of the back or seat to be covered. This will show the size and shape to be worked, although it is wise to make the embroidered area slightly larger, to allow for padding.

When a kit is being used, it will contain a pattern which can be used as a guide, allowing a little extra for the thickness of the seat padding.

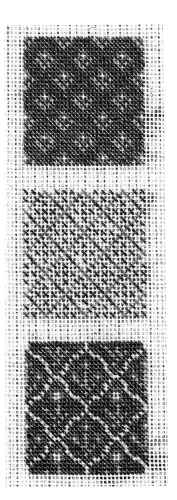

Fig 5.1 **Designs for chair canvaswork seats**

Similarly, a pattern will be included or can be made if using instructions from a book. Methods of making simple chairs of the period are shown later in this chapter (*see* page 77).

Working method

1 Make a paper pattern to the required size.

2 Mount the canvas or evenweave fabric into a frame and, using the pattern, mark the required shape with the soluble fabric pen.

3 Refer to the required chart and, beginning at the centre of the lower edge, work the design in tent stitch. For 18-count canvas use three strands of stranded cotton; for 22- or 24-count canvas use two strands; for 32-, 35- or 40- evenweave use one strand.

4 Work the design first, then fill in the background colour. The colour of the background can be altered to your choice.

5 When the embroidery is complete, remove the fabric from the frame.

6 Make up as directed by the kit maker or as directed on page 77.

Canvas Cushions

Materials

For each chair back, seat or footstool

Canvas or evenweave linen: 100mm (4in) square

The patterns can all be worked on single thread canvas: 22, 24 or 18 count. Alternatively, a smaller pattern can be achieved by using evenweave linen 32, 35 or 40 count.

Lightweight silk or cotton fabric (to match chosen background colour): 100mm (4in) square

Stranded cottons as listed in colour key

Tapestry needle: No. 24 or 26

Soluble embroidery pen

PVA fabric glue

Size

As desired

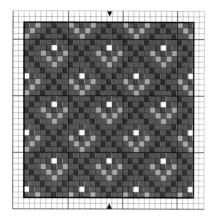

Fig 5.2 **Chart for Design 1**

Canvaswork Cushion – Design 1

		Skeins	DMC	Anchor	Madeira
	Dark red	1	815	43	0512
	Light red	1	666	9046	0210
	Yellow	1	745	300	0111
	Light green	1	3347	886	2205
	Dark blue	1	311	147	1006

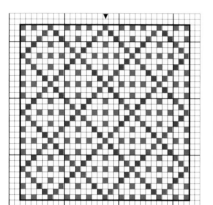

Fig 5.3 **Chart for Design 2**

Canvaswork Cushion – Design 2

		Skeins	DMC	Anchor	Madeira
	Dark red	1	815	43	0512
	Light red	1	666	9046	0210
	Yellow	1	745	300	0111
	Dark blue	1	311	147	1006

Fig 5.4 **Chart for Design 3**

Canvaswork Cushion – Design 3

		Skeins	DMC	Anchor	Madeira
	Light red	1	666	9046	0210
	Yellow	1	745	300	0111
	Light green	1	3347	886	2205
	Dark green	1	3345	888	2103

Fig 5.5 **Chair and footstool using the slips motifs**

Additional canvaswork patterns can be used for chair covers and footstools.

Fig 5.5 shows a chair and footstool using the charts for the Slip bed hangings (*see* page 17). The chair is in the style of a set at Hardwick Hall in Derbyshire, England, and has been made very simply with available components: turned stool legs, spindles and stripwood.

The chair motifs have been worked on evenweave linen, 35 count. Instructions for making a chair and footstool are given on pages 77–80. The coloured evenweave linen ground used for the footstool is 32 count with two motifs worked.

Any of the charted designs for the Oxburgh bed hangings (*see* pages 12–16) can be used for a square footstool or placed on a chair back or seat. The evenweave required and general instructions are as given for the bed hangings.

The chart for the Scrolling Stem bedcover (*see* Fig 3.4, page 41) would be ideal for chair covers and footstools, using the stitches and 35-count evenweave indicated for that project. The general instructions for the chair covers and footstools above apply.

The designs for the Intertwined Hearts and Rose Trellis cushions are suitable for chair covers and footstools. A 24- or 22-count canvas, or 32-count evenweave linen could be substituted, and the tent stitches worked in two strands of stranded cotton.

Fig 5.6 **Detail of the Oxburgh elephant motif**

71

Florentine Designs

Florentine work was popular from the mid-sixteenth century, continuing into the following centuries, sometimes referred to as flame stitch because of the way the colours are arranged on curved and zigzag patterns (*see* Fig 5.7). The secret of success lies in the choice of colours, usually five or seven; three or five of one range contrasted with two from another range. For miniature work, a 40-count evenweave needs to be used so that the threads will cover the fabric and the scale will be right.

If using a coarser fabric, the number of sewing threads will need to be increased until the stitches cover the fabric adequately.

Working method

1 Mark the required size of the chair back, seat or footstool on the fabric with tacking stitches and mount the fabric into a small card frame.

2 Using one strand of stranded cotton and straight stitches as indicated in Fig 5.8, begin a row of the design in the centre. Place the

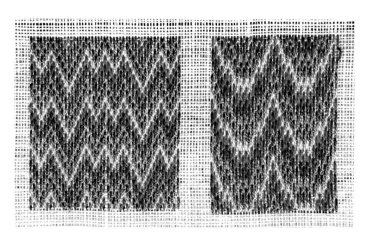

Fig 5.7 **Florentine designs**

Florentine Designs

Materials

For each chair back, seat or footstool

Evenweave linen (40 count): 100mm (4in) square

Lightweight silk or cotton fabric to match main colour: 100mm (4in) square

Stranded cottons: 5 or 7 colours, as desired

Tapestry needle: No. 26 or 28

PVA fabric glue

Size

As desired

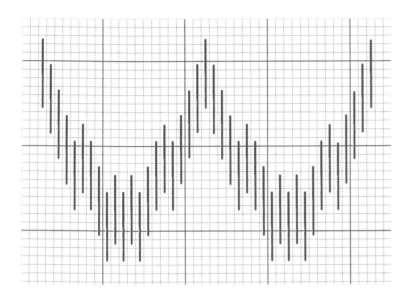

Fig 5.8 **Charts for the Florentine designs**

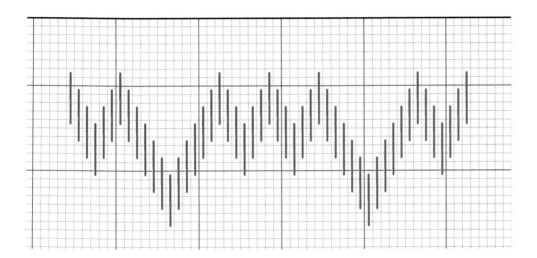

middle of an arch or a point in the centre and work towards the outer edge. Return to the centre and work the other half of the row towards the edge. Please note with the arched design that most stitches are over four threads and back under one, but some are back under two threads. In the pointed design, all the stitches are over

three threads and back under one.

3 Continue to work the remaining rows until the required area is covered.

4 When the embroidery is complete, remove the fabric from the frame.

5 Make up as directed by the kit maker or as directed on page 77.

Blackwork Designs

These designs were also traditionally worked in dark red or blue as well as in black and look very handsome as chair backs, seats and footstools. The design shown as a footstool in Fig 5.9 is typical of the late sixteenth and early seventeenth centuries. Fig 4.19 (*see* page 63), the chart for the floral hearts cushion, could also be adapted as it is an all-over design.

Fig 5.9 **Blackwork footstool**

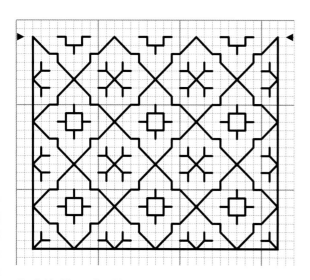

Fig 5.10 **Chart for Blackwork footstool**

Working method

1 Mark the required size on the fabric with tacking stitches.

2 Mount the fabric into a small card frame.

3 Using backstitch and one strand of thread throughout, begin to stitch in the centre of the top or lower edge.

4 Continue with the pattern until the required size and shape has been worked.

5 When the embroidery is complete, remove the fabric from the frame.

6 Make up as directed by the kit maker or as directed on page 77.

Blackwork Designs

Materials

For each chair back, seat or footstool

Evenweave linen (32, 35 or 40 count): 100mm (4in) square

Lightweight silk or cotton fabric to match main colour: 100mm (4in) square

Stranded, sewing or machine embroidery cotton in desired colour

Tapestry needle: No. 26 or 28

PVA fabric glue

Size

38 x 22mm (1¼ x ⅞in), or as desired

74

Crewelwork Designs

The simple tree of life form is shown here within three shapes. The tall rectangle would suit the high back of a seventeenth-century chair. The square version is for a seat or a smaller chair back, or for a square footstool. The wide rectangle is for a long footstool. The patterns given for the Crewelwork cushions, (*see* Fig 4.22, page 65), can also be used for chair backs, seats and footstools.

Working method

1 Transfer the required design from Fig 5.12 on to the centre of the fabric. Either trace the design with a fabric pencil or pen or use the photocopy method (*see* page 143).

2 Mount the fabric into a small card frame.

3 Refer to colour and stitch guide, Fig 5.13, and work the embroidery using back stitch and French knots with one strand of stranded cotton.

4 When the embroidery is complete, remove the fabric from the frame.

5 Make up as directed by the kit maker or as directed on page 77.

Fig 5.11 **Crewelwork chair and footstool**

Crewelwork Designs

Materials

For each chair back, seat or footstool

Lightweight silk or cotton fabric: 100mm (4in) square

Stranded cottons as listed in colour key

Embroidery needle: No. 10

PVA fabric glue

Size

As desired

Crewelwork designs

		Skeins	DMC	Anchor	Madeira
	Dark green	1	937	268	1504
	Mid green	1	3053	260	1603
	Light green	1	3013	854	1605
	Dark red	1	815	43	0512

Fig 5.12 **Patterns for the Crewelwork chair covers (above) and footstool cover (right)**

Fig 5.13 **Colour guide and stitch diagram for the Crewelwork chair covers (left) and footstool cover (below)**

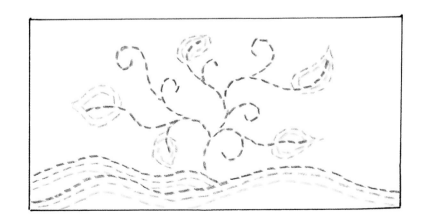

Fig 5.14 **Covering a chair seat or back**

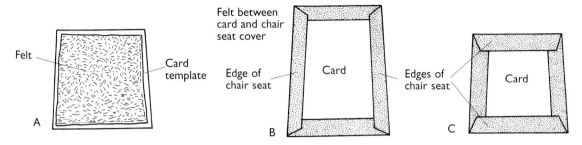

Covering a Chair Seat or Back

1 Cut a template from thin card to the exact size of the chair seat or back.

2 Cut a piece of felt slightly smaller and secure to the card with a spot of glue (*see* Fig 5.14A).

3 Using PVA fabric glue, turn the edges of the fabric or embroidered seat cover on each side (*see* Fig 5.14B). Allow to dry.

4 Trim a little excess fabric from the corners and glue the front and back under in the same way (*see* Fig 5.14C).

5 Glue the covered seat or back into position.

Make a Simple Chair

The measurements given for the wood required are given in metric and imperial as suppliers seem to use both. Remember to use one or the other, do not mix both as they are not intended to be interchangeable.

NB: The general 'Covering a Chair Seat or Back' instructions above do not apply when making the following chairs from scratch.

Sixteenth-century chair

Working method

1 Using Fig 5.15 as a pattern, trim the stool legs to the height indicated.

2 Cut two pieces from the 6mm (¼in) stripwood for the back legs and support.

Sixteenth- and seventeenth-century chairs

Materials
For each chair back, seat or footstool

2 turned stool legs

Stripwood: 200mm (8in) of 6 x 6mm (¼ x ¼in) square

Flat stripwood: 100mm (4in) of 50 x 3mm (2 x ⅛in)

Dowelling or turned components: 150mm (6in) x 2mm (¹⁄₁₆in)

2 turned knobs for top of back (optional)

6mm (¼in)-thick foam padding or wadding

Wood glue

Stain or varnish as desired

Size

See Fig 5.15 for exact size

77

Fig 5.15 **Making a simple sixteenth-century chair**

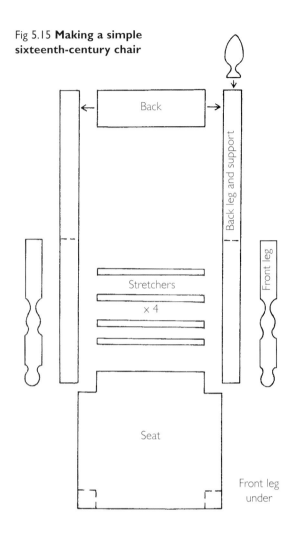

Back

Back leg and support

Front leg

Stretchers

x 4

Seat

Front leg under

3 Cut the back and seat from the 50 x 3mm (2 x ⅛in) flat stripwood as indicated on the pattern.

4 Glue the front legs under the seat as indicated. Allow to dry.

5 Glue the seat to the back legs so that the seat is level. Allow to dry.

6 Stain or varnish as required, including stretchers not yet fitted.

7 Cut a piece of foam or wadding to fit the seat and secure in place with a small spot of glue.

8 Cover a card back with fabric or embroidery, taking the fabric to the reverse side and securing with glue, and glue to wooden back.

9 Glue the back into position on the back supports. The addition of the fabric should make the back wide enough to fit on the front of the supports (*see* Fig 5.5).

10 Cover the seat area with fabric or embroidery by snipping into the corners of the fabric and fitting around the legs and to the underneath of the seat. Glue the front and back edges first and allow them to dry. Then secure the sides.

11 Finally, trim the stretchers to fit the front, back and side openings between the legs. Small turned components can be used, if desired, instead of dowelling.

Seventeenth-century chair

A later style of chair, with a higher back, can be made using Fig 5.16 as a pattern. The materials and size are as for the Sixteenth-century chair above.

Working method

1 Using Fig 5.16 as a pattern, cut out the parts as in steps 1, 2 and 3 above.

2 Assemble as in steps 4, 5 and 6 above. Stain and varnish as required.

3 Cover the seat as in step 10 above.

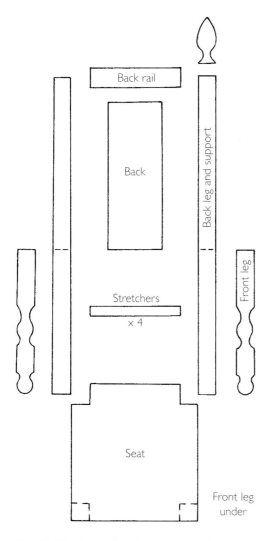

Fig 5.16 **Making a simple seventeenth-century chair**

4 Cover the back with fabric or embroidery as above and glue into place at the centre back of the seat and fit the back rail to the upper edge of the back and between the back supports.

5 Fit the stretchers to the front, back and side openings between the legs.

Making up a footstool

Rectangular and square footstools

1 Cut a template from thin card to the required shape and size. This needs to be slightly smaller than the embroidered area to allow for the padding: (*see* Fig 5.17A).

2 Cut a piece of felt slightly smaller than the card and secure it to the card with a spot of PVA fabric glue (*see* Fig 5.17B).

3 Lay the embroidered fabric over the card and secure the edges to the underside of the card. Fix two opposite sides first and allow to dry. Then fix the two remaining sides (*see* Fig 5.17C).

4 Now measure the size of the covered stool top and cut a piece of 3–5mm (⅛–¼in)-thick flat stripwood to extend 1mm around all sides.

5 Glue four small wooden beads or stool legs to the underneath (*see* Fig 5.17D). Stain and varnish as desired.

6 Finally, glue the covered stool top into position (*see* Fig 5.17E).

Round footstools

When using a commercial kit, follow the maker's instructions. Alternatively, make your own footstool from a self-covering button mould and 3mm (⅛in)-thick flat stripwood.

1 Using the button mould as a guide, draw around it to make a circle on the stripwood.

2 Cut out the circle of wood: trim roughly to shape with a craft knife and sand down to a circle.

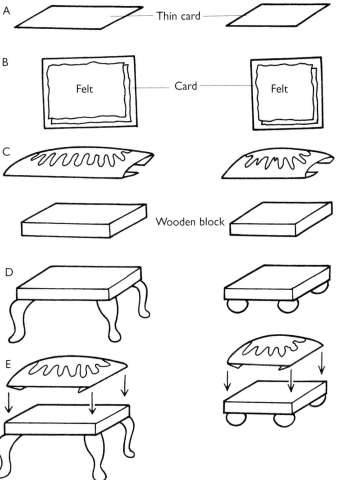

Fig 5.17 **Making up a square or rectangular footstool**

A — Thin card

B Felt — Card — Felt

C

Wooden block

D

E

6 Work a gathering thread around the edge and place the embroidered circle over the button mould (*see* Fig 5.18C). When it is in the correct position, draw up and fasten off the gathering thread (*see* Fig 5.18D).

7 Finally, glue the covered button mould into position on the wooden stool base (*see* Fig 5.18E).

3 Glue three wooden beads to the underneath of the wooden circle.

4 Stain and varnish as desired.

5 Cut a template from thin card the same size as the button mould (*see* Fig 5.18A). Lay the template on the embroidered piece, making sure the design is central, and trim the fabric around the edge to about 10mm (⅜ in) wider all round (*see* Fig 5.18B).

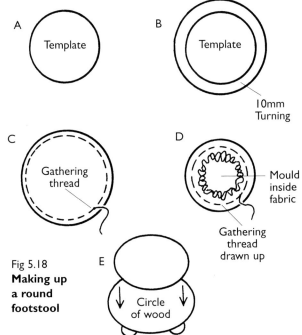

A Template

B Template — 10mm Turning

C Gathering thread

D Mould inside fabric — Gathering thread drawn up

E Circle of wood

Fig 5.18 **Making up a round footstool**

6 Screens

During the sixteenth and seventeenth centuries, many large wealthy houses would have had a built-in screen in the main hall. Usually, this would have been a decorated wooden structure inside the main entrance often forming a 'corridor' and isolating the kitchen area as a fire precaution. Sometimes the space above was used as a minstrels' gallery.

Folding screens may have been used in smaller rooms, near the door, to prevent a draught. Later in the seventeenth century, pole screens were used to protect the face from the direct heat of a fire. I have also included fire screens as old embroidery was often re-mounted and used for this purpose in later centuries.

Slips Three-fold Screen

This pretty little screen is based on the Slips bed hangings (*see* page 17).

Fig 6.1 **Slips three-fold screen**

Slips Three-fold Screen

Materials

Evenweave linen or cotton (35 count):
   200 x 150mm (8 x 6in)
Stranded cotton as listed in colour key
Tapestry needle: No. 26
Tacking cotton

Stripwood:
   1 piece: 450mm long x 45mm wide
     x 3mm thick (18 x 1½ x ⅛in)
   3 pieces: 450mm long x 6mm wide
     x 3mm thick (18 x ¼ x ⅛in)
Backing: Vilene, thin leather or felt,
     200 x 150mm (8 x 6in)
PVA wood glue

Size

Each panel
100 x 32mm (4 x 1¼in)

Each motif
28 stitches square

Working method

1 Using tacking cotton, mark the size of the three panels as above. Place the panels side by side on the linen leaving 25mm (1in) between the panels.

2 Mount the fabric in a small rectangular frame.

3 Refer to the chart, Fig 2.11 (*see* page 21) and the colour key (right). Using the desired motifs, work the embroidery in tent stitch over one thread of the fabric. Use one strand of stranded cotton.

4 When the embroidery is complete, remove the fabric from the frame.

5 Make up as directed on page 90.

Slips Three-fold Screen

		Skeins	DMC	Anchor	Madeira
	Dark blue	1	797	147	0912
	Mid blue	1	799	145	0910
	Light blue	1	800	159	1002
	Gold	1	725	305	0106
	Bright yellow	1	307	289	0104
	Light yellow	1	3078	292	0102
	Cream	1	739	1009	2014
	Purple	1	791	123	0904
	Dark mauve	1	553	99	0712
	Light mauve	1	554	96	0711
	Dark pink	1	892	28	0412
	Mid pink	1	3326	36	0606
	Light pink	1	818	271	0608
	Red	1	321	47	0510
	Dark red	1	815	43	0512
	Dark green	1	500	879	1705
	Mid green	1	368	214	1310
	Light green	1	369	1043	1309
	Dark grey green	1	502	876	1703
	Light grey green	1	504	1042	1701
	Dark olive green	1	3011	924	1607
	Light olive green	1	3013	854	1605

Millefleurs Screen

In addition to the three fold screen shown in Fig 6.2, this project can be used for a wall hanging by omitting the spaces between the panels. The design is based on a Franco-Nederlandish woven tapestry from the early sixteenth century, which can be found in the Burrell Collection in Glasgow.

Fig 6.2 **Millefleurs three-fold screen**

Working method

1 Using tacking cotton, mark the size of the three panels (*see* below). Place the panels side by side on the linen leaving 25mm (1in) between the panels.

2 Mount the fabric in a small rectangular frame.

3 Refer to the chart, (*see* Figs 6.4A, B and C, page 84–5), and work the embroidery in tent stitch over one thread of the fabric. Use one strand of stranded cotton. Work the motifs first and then fill in the ground colours.

4 When the embroidery is complete, remove the fabric from the frame.

5 Make up as directed on page 90.

Millefleurs Screen

Materials

Evenweave linen or cotton (35 count):
    250 x 200mm (10 x 8in)
Stranded cotton as listed in colour key
Tapestry needle: No. 26
Tacking cotton

Stripwood:
    1 piece: 450mm long x 60mm wide
        x 3mm thick (18 x 2¼ x ⅛in)
    3 pieces: 450mm long x 6mm wide
        x 3mm thick (18 x ¼ x ⅛in)
    Backing: Vilene or thin leather,
        200 x 150mm (8 x 6in)
    PVA wood glue

Size

Each panel

165 x 60 stitches
120 x 45 mm (4¾ x 1¾in)

Fig 6.3 **Millefleurs screen**

Fig 6.4A **Chart for lefthand panel of Millefleurs screen**

Fig 6.4B **Chart for centre panel of Millefleurs screen**

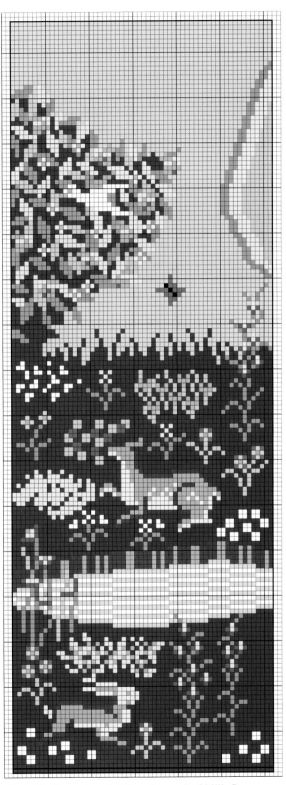

Fig 6.4C **Chart for righthand panel of Millefleurs screen**

Millefleurs Screen

		Skeins	DMC	Anchor	Madeira
	Dark brown	I	898	360	2006
	Mid brown	I	433	371	2008
	Light brown	I	841	378	1911
	Cream	I	677	886	2207
	Dark green	I	500	879	1705
	Mid green	I	502	876	1703
	Light green	I	504	1042	1701
	Yellow green	I	472	264	1414
	Peach	I	353	868	0304
	Orange	I	741	314	0201
	Red	I	321	47	0510
	White	I	Blanc	White	White
	Light blue	I	827	9159	1014
	Mid blue	I	798	137	0911
	Black	I	310	Black	Black

Strapwork Pole and Fire Screen

The use of the strapwork device as a design motif was extremely popular in the sixteenth and seventeenth centuries. It can be found decorating textiles, architecture and as a basis for knot gardens. The intertwining lines appear to pass over and under one another, an effect achieved here by changing the shade.

Fig 6.5 **Strapwork pole and fire screens**

Strapwork Pole and Fire Screens

Materials

Pole screen: evenweave linen (35 count): 75mm (3in)
  square

Fire screen: single-thread canvas (22 count): 100mm
  (4in) square.

Stranded cottons as listed in colour key

Tapestry needle: No. 24 or 26

Tacking cotton

Materials for making up: *see* pages 92–3.

Size

Pole screen: 33 x 25mm (1¼ x 1in)

Fire screen: 50 x 40mm (2 x 1½in)

Both: 45 x 35 stitches

Fig 6.6 **Detail of strapwork
screens**

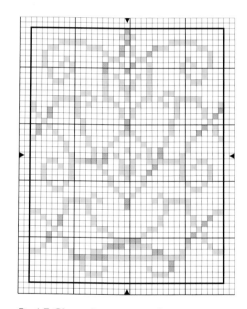

Fig 6.7 **Chart for strapwork
screens**

Working method

1 Using tacking cotton, mark the outer edge of the screen (*see* page 140).

2 Mount the fabric/canvas in a card frame or small rectangular frame.

3 Using the chart, Fig 6.7, work the embroidery in tent stitch over one thread of the fabric for the pole screen, or two strands for the fire screen. Work the motifs first and then fill in the background colours.

4 When the embroidery is complete, remove the fabric from the frame.

5 Make up as directed on pages 92–3.

Strapwork Pole and Fire Screens

		Skeins	DMC	Anchor	Madeira
	Gold	1	725	305	0106
	Dark gold	1	832	907	2202
	Blue	1	799	145	0910

Water Garden Pole and Fire Screens

The design for these items has been adapted from a Scottish bed valance dated 1594. It shows a water feature within a garden setting, a very popular subject from the sixteenth to the eighteenth century (*see* Figs 6.8 and 6.9).

Fig 6.8 **Water Garden pole and fire screens**

Fig 6.9 **Chart for the Water Garden screens**

The materials, sizes and working method are the same as given for the Strapwork pole and fire screens (*see* page 86). Refer to the chart (*see* Fig 6.9).

Water Garden Pole and Fire Screens

		Skeins	DMC	Anchor	Madeira
	Dark green	1	500	879	1705
	Mid green	1	502	876	1703
	Light green	1	504	1042	1701
	Cream	1	3047	886	2205
	Brown	1	839	1050	1913
	Red	1	321	47	0510
	Pink	1	353	868	0304
	Light blue	1	799	145	0910
	Orange	1	741	314	0201
	White	1	Blanc	White	White

Persian Pole and Fire Screens

Imported woven or tufted carpets were the height of luxury, available only to the most wealthy and prestigious. They would have been displayed on a table or hung on the wall.

The design for these screens (*see* Figs 6.10 and 6.11) has been taken from a Persian carpet from the seventeenth century which can be found in the Victoria and Albert Museum in London.

Fig 6.10 **Persian pole and fire screens**

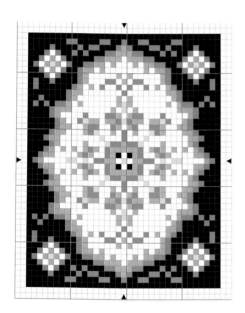

The materials, sizes and working method are the same as given for the Strapwork pole and fire screens (*see* page 86).

Refer to the chart (*see* Fig 6.11).

Fig 6.11 **Chart for the Persian screens**

Persian Pole and Fire Screens

		Skeins	DMC	Anchor	Madeira
	Blue	1	517	169	1107
	Pink	1	335	38	0610
	Yellow	1	743	305	0113
	Black	1	310	Black	Black
	White	1	Blanc	White	White

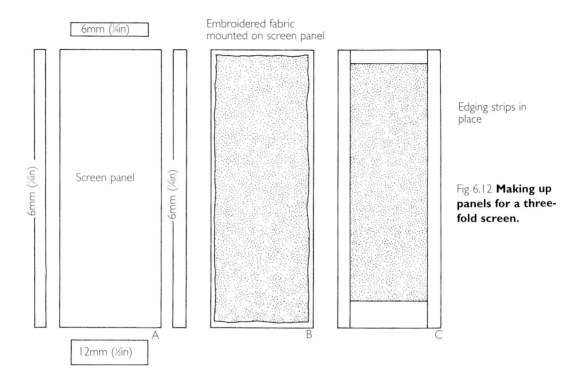

6mm (¼in)

Embroidered fabric
mounted on screen panel

6mm (¼in)

Screen panel

6mm (¼in)

Edging strips in
place

A

B

C

12mm (½in)

Fig 6.12 **Making up
panels for a three-
fold screen.**

Making up a
three-fold screen

1 Stain and varnish all stripwood as desired.

2 Using the widest stripwood for the screen panels, cut three pieces:

Slip screens: 120mm (4¾in) long.

Millefleurs screen: 140mm (5½in) long (*see* Fig 6.12A).

3 Cover the front of each panel of stripwood with a thin layer of PVA glue and allow to dry completely.

4 Place the embroidered panels into position on the dry glue. Leave 6mm (¼in) at the top

and 12mm (½in) at the lower edge for the edging strips (*see* Fig 6.12B).

5 With a warm iron, seal each edge of the embroidery in turn to bond the fabric to the wood. Do the two long sides first, slightly stretching the fabric so that it lays flat.

6 Cut six lengths of the 6mm (¼in) stripwood to the same length as the screen panels, and, using wood glue sparingly, glue them into place each side of the panels.

7 Cut three pieces each from 6mm (¼in) and 12mm (½in) stripwood to fit between the side strips at the top and lower edges of each panel.

8 Glue into position (*see* Fig 6.12C).

Assembling and hinging the screen

1 Place the leather or vilene backing face down on to the work surface. The vilene can be coloured with paint or dye first if required. Do not cut to size or shape: the backing should be larger than the completed screen.

2 Spread PVA glue sparingly on the back of the second and third screen panels and place them side by side close together on the backing (*see* Fig 6.13A). Allow to dry.

3 Place the first screen panel face down on top of the second panel.

4 Spread glue sparingly over the backing beside the two panels, and fold the backing up and over the back of the first panel (*see* Fig 6.13B). Ensure that the backing is fixed to the side edges of the first and second panel to form a hinge (*see* Fig 6.13C). Allow to dry completely.

5 Finally, with a sharp craft knife, cut away the surplus backing from around the edges of the completed screen.

The screen will now fold into a zigzag to stand (*see* Fig 6.13D).

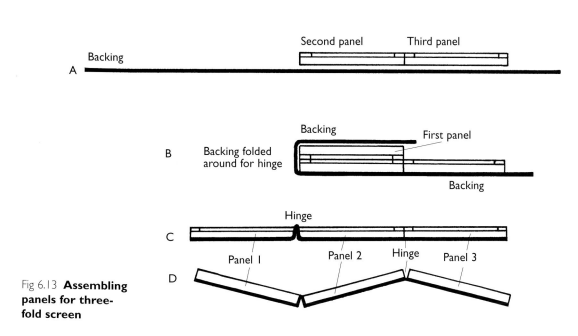

Fig 6.13 **Assembling panels for three-fold screen**

Making up a pole screen

If you are using a commercially made kit, follow the manufacturers directions. To make your own, follow the instructions below.

Working method

1 Make the frame for the screen by cutting the moulding, with mitred corners as shown (*see* Fig 6.15). The measurements of the inside edges are the same as the outer edges of the embroidery: i.e. the inner opening of the frame fits around the completed embroidery.

2 Glue the corners of the moulding together and allow to dry.

3 Spread a thin, smooth layer of glue on to the card surface.

4 Lay the embroidered fabric into position on the card, ensuring that the embroidery is square. Lay the frame over the embroidery to check. When satisfied, press the embroidery gently on to the glued surface to secure. Allow to dry.

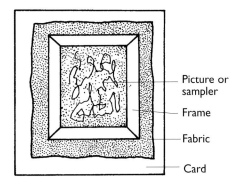

Fig 6.14 Mounting a picture in moulding with no rebate

Pole Screens

Materials

Mounting card: 100mm (4in) square
Miniature picture-frame moulding: 30mm (12in)
Ready-turned spindle or dowelling: 3mm (⅛in) diameter x 100mm (4in) long
Stripwood: 3mm (⅛in) thick x 25mm (1in) square
Wooden beads x 3
PVA wood glue
Stain and varnish as desired

Fig 6.15 **Making up a pole screen**

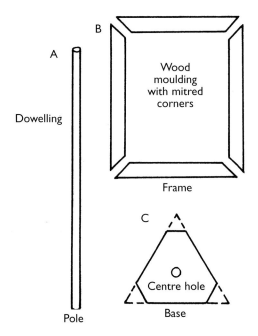

5 Using glue very sparingly, attach the frame to the mounted embroidery.

6 Finally, with a sharp craft knife, cut away the surplus card and fabric from around the edges of the frame.

7 Cut the pole screen base from the small square of stripwood (*see* Fig 6.15). Drill a small hole in the centre to take the pole.

8 Glue three wooden beads to the underside.

9 Glue the pole into the hole in the base and the embroidered screen into position on the front of the pole.

Making up a fire screen

If using a commercially made kit, follow the manufacturers instructions. To make your own, follow the instructions below.

Working method

1 Make the outer frame and mount the fabric as directed in steps 1 to 6 above, for the pole screen (*see* Fig 6.16A).

2 Make the two feet from the stripwood, each 15mm (¹⁄₂in) long. Shape the upper ends as shown (*see* Fig 6.16B).

3 Glue the feet into position as indicated (*see* Fig 6.16C).

Fire Screens

Materials

Mounting card: 100mm (4in) square

Miniature picture-frame moulding: 30mm (12in)

Stripwood: 5 x 5 x 40mm (³⁄₁₆ x ³⁄₁₆ x 1¹⁄₂in)

PVA glue

Stain and varnish as required

Fig 6.16 **Making up a fire screen**

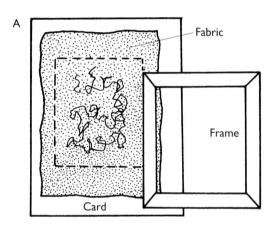

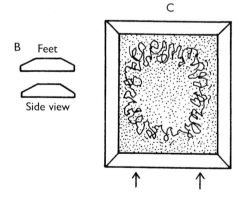

7 Pictures and samplers

Small pictures became fashionable during the seventeenth century. By this time, many wealthy houses had wood panelling in the main rooms and no longer wished to cover their walls with large wall hangings and woven tapestries. The small pictures were created using several techniques: canvaswork, tapestry weaving, raised embroidery (later known as stumpwork), silk embroidery and beadwork. The subjects chosen ranged from Royal personages to biblical stories and legends, and were often depicted in small scenes within a landscape.

Samplers during the sixteenth and seventeenth century were originally a method of recording patterns; almost a substitute for books. They were not for display, but to be rolled up in the work box for reference. Very few survive that are dated to the sixteenth century.

Samplers from the seventeenth century seem to have become a schoolroom exercise as the patterns worked on them are those used during the reign of Elizabeth I. By the middle of the century a sampler was the first sewing task in a young lady's education.

Samplers were often long and narrow, being worked on a length of linen woven especially for the purpose. There were two main types: the band sampler and the spot sampler. Band samplers began with simple patterned borders, progressing through a range of colours with increasingly complex techniques and designs, finishing with whitework and Reticella bands (an early form of substitute lace, worked on withdrawn threads in buttonhole stitch).

Spot samplers contained isolated motifs: flowers, animals, birds, mythical beasts, insects, geometric designs and examples of all-over patterns for use on chairs and stools etc. Samplers can be seen in many museums, books and collections.

The samplers featured here are framed as they would appear in a later or museum setting. They could be unframed and partially rolled in a workbox.

'Moses in the Bulrushes' and 'Royal' Pictures

Both of these designs (*see* Figs 7.1A and 7.1B) are typical of the fashion in the middle of the seventeenth century.

Fig 7.1A **'Moses in the Bulrushes' picture, worked on 40-count fabric**

'Moses in the Bulrushes' and 'Royal' Pictures

Materials

Evenweave linen (35 or 40 count): 75mm (3in) square

Stranded cotton as listed in colour key

Tapestry needle: No. 26

Mounting card: 2mm (1⁄10in) thick, 75mm (3in) square

PVA glue

Miniature picture-frame moulding: 30cm (12in)

Fig 7.1B **'Royal' picture, worked on 35-count fabric**

Size

40-count fabric: 50 x 40 stitches, 31 x 24mm (1¼ x 1in)

35-count fabric: 37 x 30mm (1½ x 1⅛in)

Working method

1 Mount the fabric in a card frame or small rectangular frame (*see* page 137).

2 Each square on the charts (*see* Figs 7.2 and 7.3) represents one stitch. Use one strand of stranded cotton or metallic thread and tent stitch throughout. Begin working the design either from a corner or the centre. Stitch the main elements of the design first, then fill in the lightest green and the sky.

3 When the embroidery is complete, remove the fabric from the frame.

4 Make up as directed on page 104.

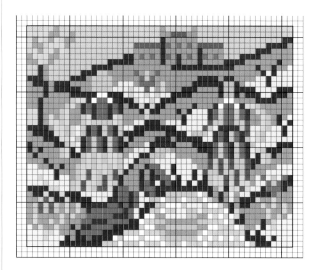

Fig 7.2 **Chart for the 'Moses in the Bulrushes' picture**

'Moses in the Bulrushes' Picture

		Skeins	DMC	Anchor	Madeira
	Dark brown	1	839	1050	1913
	Light brown	1	841	378	1911
	Gold	1	725	305	0106
	Orange	1	742	303	0107
	Dark green	1	500	879	1705
	Mid green	1	502	876	1703
	Light green	1	504	1042	1701
	Yellow green	1	472	264	1414
	Red	1	321	47	0510
	Dark blue	1	820	134	0904
	Mid blue	1	798	137	0911
	Light blue	1	800	159	1002
	Flesh	1	950	376	2309
	White	1	Blanc	White	White

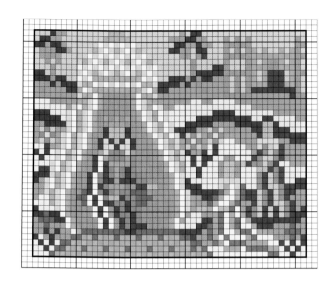

Fig 7.3 **Chart for the 'Royal' picture**

'Royal' Picture

		Skeins	DMC	Anchor	Madeira
	Gold	I	Metallic	Metallic	Metallic
	Dark gold	I	832	907	2202
	Yellow	I	744	301	0110
	Dark brown	I	839	1050	1913
	Light brown	I	841	378	1911
	Orange	I	740	316	0202
	Red	I	321	47	0510
	Dark green	I	500	879	1705
	Mid green	I	502	876	1703
	Light green	I	504	1042	1701
	Flesh	I	950	376	2309
	Dark blue	I	820	134	0904
	Mid blue	I	799	145	0910
	Light blue	I	800	159	1002

Stumpwork Picture

Raised embroidery became known as stumpwork in the late nineteenth century. It uses a group of techniques which give a raised and detached effect: detached and surface buttonhole stitch, satin stitch, French knots, tiny pieces of applied canvaswork, beads etc. It was worked by young girls and was most popular between 1650 and 1680.

The typical design used here (*see* Fig 7.4) shows a lady playing a musical instrument in a garden setting surrounded by flower motifs.

Fig 7.4 **Stumpwork picture**

Stumpwork Picture

Materials

Cream satin or silk: 100mm (4in) square
Stranded cottons as listed in colour key
Embroidery/crewel needle: No. 10
Mounting card: 2mm (1/16 in) thick, 100mm (4in) square
PVA glue
Miniature picture-frame moulding: 30cm (12in)

Size

32 x 25mm (1¼ x 1in)

Fig 7.5 **Pattern for the Stumpwork picture**

Working method

1 Transfer the pattern (*see* Fig 7.5) to the fabric using one of the methods described in Chapter 12 (*see* page 142). Your fabric is probably thin enough to see through, allowing you to trace the design on to the fabric with a fabric pen or pencil.

2 Mount the fabric in a card frame or small rectangular frame (*see* page 137).

3 Refer to the diagram (*see* Fig 7.6) and work the embroidery using one strand of stranded cotton. The dots indicate French knots to give the effect of raised stitches; the straight parallel lines indicate satin stitch; and the remaining broken lines indicate backstitch.

4 When the embroidery is complete, remove the fabric from the frame.

5 Make up as directed on page 104.

Fig 7.6 **Stitch and colour guide for the Stumpwork picture**

Stumpwork Picture

		Skeins	DMC	Anchor	Madeira
	Dark brown	I	839	1050	1913
	Light brown	I	612	888	2108
	Dark green	I	937	268	1504
	Mid green	I	906	256	1410
	Light green	I	472	264	1414
	Red	I	321	47	0510
	Dark pink	I	352	9	0303
	Light pink	I	353	868	0304
	Flesh	I	543	933	1909
	Dark blue	I	517	169	1107
	Light blue	I	807	168	1109
	Yellow	I	972	298	0107

Fig 7.7 **Elizabethan sampler**

Elizabethan Sampler

The designs used on this sampler (*see* Fig 7.7) are based on the Jane Bostocke sampler, dated 1598, which can be seen in London's Victoria and Albert Museum. The original is worked on linen and embroidered with silk, seed pearls and metal thread.

Working method

1 Mount the fabric in a card frame or small rectangular frame (*see* page 137).

2 With tacking cotton, mark the vertical and horizontal centres.

3 Each square on the chart (*see* Fig 7.8) represents one stitch. The solid squares are tent stitch and the lines require a back stitch in the direction indicated on the chart. Use one strand of stranded cotton throughout.

4 Begin with the top plant motif, then the Hart (deer) which will enable the positioning of the other motifs.

5 When the embroidery is complete, remove the fabric from the frame.

6 Make up as directed on page 104.

Elizabethan Sampler

Materials

Evenweave linen (40 count): 100mm (4in) square

Stranded cotton as listed in colour key

Tapestry needle: No. 26 or 28

Mounting card: 2mm (⅒in) thick, 100mm (4in) square

PVA glue

Miniature picture-frame moulding: 30cm (12in)

Size

70 x 50 stitches, 42 x 30mm (1⅝ x 1³⁄₁₆in)

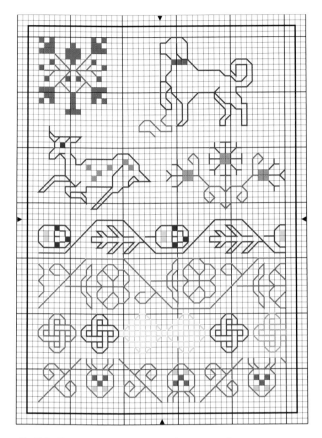

Fig 7.8 **Chart for the Elizabethan sampler**

Band Sampler

The patterns used for this sampler (*see* Fig 7.9) are based on those used during the first half of the seventeenth century.

Fig 7.9 **Band sampler**

Elizabethan, Band and Spot Motif Samplers

		Skeins	DMC	Anchor	Madeira
	Dark green	I	937	268	1504
	Mid green	I	472	264	1414
	Red	I	321	47	0510
	Pink	I	899	66	0609
	Yellow	I	743	305	0113
	Dark blue	I	820	134	0904
	Light blue	I	813	161	1013
	Dark brown	I	839	1050	1913
	Light brown	I	612	888	2108

Band Sampler

Materials

Evenweave linen (40 count): 180 x 75mm (7 x 3in)

Stranded cotton as listed in colour key

Tapestry needle: No. 26 or 28

Mounting card: 2mm (1⁄16 in) thick, 180 x 75mm (7 x 3in)

PVA glue

Miniature picture-frame moulding: 30cm (12in)

Size

180 x 30 stitches, 110 x 17mm (4⅜ x ⅝in)

Fig 7.10 **Chart for the Band sampler**

Working method

As for the Elizabethan Sampler (*see* page 100). Begin stitching at the top, using the chart (*see* Fig 7.10).

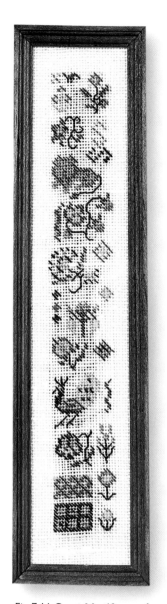

Fig 7.11 **Spot Motif sampler**

Spot Motif Sampler

Spot Motif Sampler

Materials

Evenweave linen (35 count): 180 x 75mm (7 x 3in)

Stranded cotton as listed in colour key

Tapestry needle: No. 26 or 28

Mounting card: 2mm (¹⁄₁₀ in) thick, 180 x 75mm (7 x 3in)

PVA glue

Miniature picture-frame moulding: 30cm (12in)

Size

156 x 25 stitches, 110 x 17mm (4⅜ x ⅝in)

Fig 7.12 **Chart for the Spot Motif sampler**

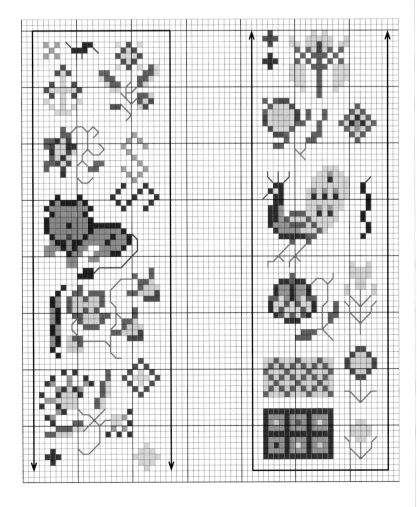

These patterns (*see* Fig 7.11) are based on mid-seventeenth-century samplers.

Working method

As for the Elizabethan sampler. Begin stitching at the top using chart (*see* Fig 7.12)

Mounting and framing pictures and samplers

Miniature picture-frame moulding comes in various sizes and some have a rebate on the reverse side to receive the mounted picture. The steps in making the frame are the same for mouldings with or without a rebate, but mounting the embroidered picture differs slightly depending on whether a rebated or flat-backed moulding is used.

Making the frame

1 Cut and mitre the moulding to the required size as shown in Fig 7.13A. The inner edges, a–a and b–b, should be the same length as the finished embroidery.

2 Carefully glue the corners of the frame, wiping away any excess glue. Allow to dry completely.

3 Stain and varnish or paint as required.

Mounting using rebated moulding

1 Cut a piece of mounting card to fit inside the rebate of the frame (*see* Fig 7.13B).

2 Cover the front of the card with a thin layer of PVA glue, wiping off any excess so the card is just tacky. Drawing the straight edge of a piece of card over the glued surface will effectively remove the excess.

3 Place the embroidery into position on the tacky card. Check that the position is correct

Fig 7.13 **Mounting a picture in rebated moulding.**

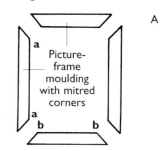

Picture-frame moulding with mitred corners

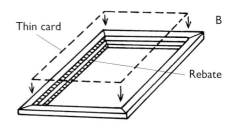

Thin card

Rebate

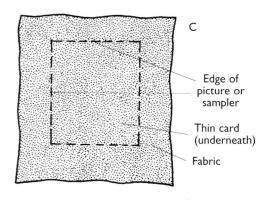

Edge of picture or sampler

Thin card (underneath)

Fabric

and gently press down gently all over (*see* Fig 7.13C). Leave to dry completely.

4 Trim away the excess fabric from around the edge.

5 Push the picture or sampler into the back of the frame and secure with narrow masking tape.

Mounting using flat-backed moulding

1 Cut a piece of mounting card 100mm (4in) square and cover it with PVA glue as described in step 2 above.

2 Place the embroidery on the tacky surface and lay the frame over it to make sure the embroidery is square. Gently push into position if necessary and then press down firmly. Allow to dry completely.

3 Glue the frame into position. Use the glue sparingly (*see* Fig 7.14). Leave to dry completely.

4 With a sharp craft knife, cut away the surplus card and fabric from around the four sides.

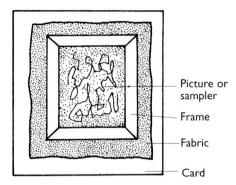

Fig 7.14 **Mounting a picture in moulding with no rebate**

8 Table carpets and wall hangings

During the sixteenth and seventeenth centuries carpets were considered too precious to be used as a floor covering. Only the households of the very wealthy could afford such an item, which was then used as a table covering for display or meetings. The table would usually have been bare at meal times, although a plain linen cloth may have been used for special functions.

The most desirable – and expensive – table carpets were imported woven tufted examples, to a traditional format of central motifs surrounded by an all-over pattern, with a decorative border to the edges.

Embroidered carpets, although prestigious, were more common. Some existing examples were probably displayed as wall hangings as they have a central pictorial design to be viewed vertically.

Fig 8.1 **From left to right: Border table carpet, Music Makers wall hanging and Emblem table carpet**

  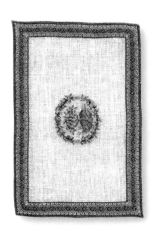

Landscape Carpet

This project is based on the Bradford table carpet which can be seen in the Victoria and Albert Museum in London. The original, dating from the late sixteenth century, has a centre with an all-over design of vines, and a border filled with various rural scenes. It is a good example of how the ladies of a great house would employ a journeyman embroiderer to prepare such an item for them, taking pictorial scenes from the books of the time and arranging them in a border. The pictures were used without any consideration of perspective or season: for example, people are larger than houses and trees are in bud, flower and fruit.

The original is quite large: 396 x 175cm (13ft x 5ft 9in).

Working method

The charts (*see* Fig 8.3) are shown as individual units which, when placed side by side, join up. This allows you to place the units in any order, or to make a carpet another size. Alternatively, refer to the photograph (*see* Fig 8.2) for placement with one of the larger units to each side.

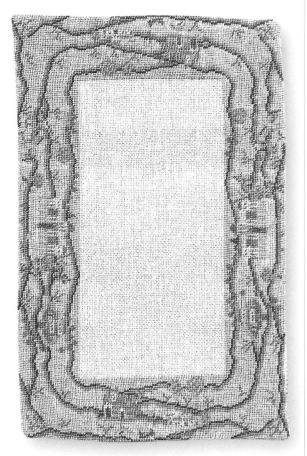

Fig 8.2 **Landscape carpet**

1 Using tacking thread, mark the size of the carpet on the linen. Do this by measuring to find an initial approximate size. Then mark the vertical and horizontal centres.

2 Mount the fabric in a small rectangular frame (*see* page 137).

Landscape Table Carpet

Materials
Evenweave linen (35 count): 250 x 150mm (10 x 6in)
Stranded cotton as listed in colour key
Tacking thread
Tapestry needle: No. 26 or 28

Size
177 x 116mm (7 x 4½in)

3 Refer to the charts (*see* Fig 8.3) and beginning in the centre of one side work the embroidery. Use one strand of stranded cotton and tent stitch throughout.

4 Add units from the charts, including the corners, until the required size is achieved. If this takes you a few threads over your original tacked outline, do not worry: this was only intended as a guide to find the centres.

5 When the embroidery is complete, remove the fabric from the frame.

6 Finish the edges as directed on page 114.

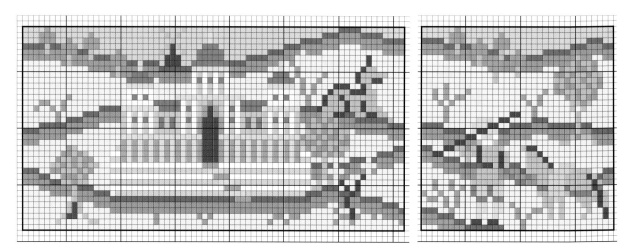

Figs 8.3A & B **Charts for Landscape table carpet**

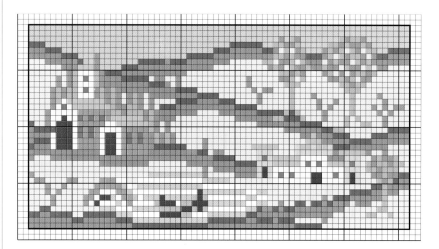

Fig 8.3C **Chart for Landscape table carpet**

Landscape Table Carpet

		Skeins	DMC	Anchor	Madeira
	Dark green	1	319	683	1313
	Mid green	1	320	216	1311
	Light green	1	369	1043	1309
	Bright green	1	905	257	1412
	Green	1	906	256	1410
	Dark brown	1	839	1050	1913
	Light brown	1	841	378	1911
	Terracotta	1	356	1013	0402
	Cream	1	739	1009	2014
	Mid cream	1	3046	887	2206
	Dark cream	1	3045	888	2103
	Dark blue	1	798	137	0911
	Light blue	1	800	159	1002
	Pink	1	3326	36	0606
	White	1	Blanc	White	White

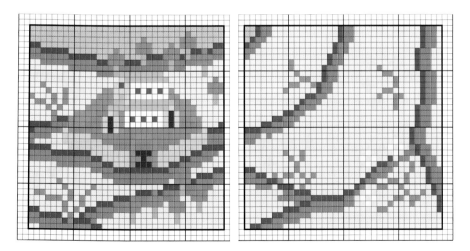

Fig 8.3D & E **Charts for Landscape table carpet**

Fig 8.4 **Emblem table carpet**

Emblem Table Carpet

The traditional format of a woven carpet has been used for this project which is based on the Gifford table carpet in the Victoria and Albert Museum, London. The original has three central roundels; two with a stag and an oak tree (the family emblem) and one with heraldic arms. The original also has an all-over pattern filling the background which has been omitted on this miniature. Dated to about 1550, the original carpet measures 554 x 142cm (18ft x 4ft 8in).

Working method

1 Prepare as step 1 for the Landscape carpet.
2 Mount the fabric in a small rectangular frame (*see* page 137).
3 Refer to chart (*see* Fig 8.5) and work the central motif using the centre tacking lines for placement. Use one thread of stranded cotton and tent stitch throughout.
4 Using the border chart (*see* Fig 8.6), begin the border in the centre of one long side. Start with the inside row of dark green stitches, leaving 30 threads of the fabric between the

Emblem Table Carpet

Materials
Evenweave linen (35 count): 250 x 180mm (10 x 7in)
Stranded cotton as listed in colour key
Tacking cotton
Tapestry needle: No. 26 or 28

Size
172 x 115mm (6¾ x 4½in)

Emblem Table Carpet

		Skeins	DMC	Anchor	Madeira
	Dark green	1	319	683	1313
	Mid green	1	470	266	1410
	Light green	1	472	264	1414
	Dark pink	1	602	63	0702
	Light pink	1	776	24	0607
	Red	1	321	47	0510
	Dark brown	1	839	1050	1913
	Light brown	1	841	378	1911
	Dark gold	1	832	907	2202
	Light gold	1	834	874	2206
	Blue	1	807	168	1109

inside of the border and the lowest stitch of the centre motif.

5 When the embroidery is complete, remove the fabric from the frame.

6 Finish the edges as directed on page 114.

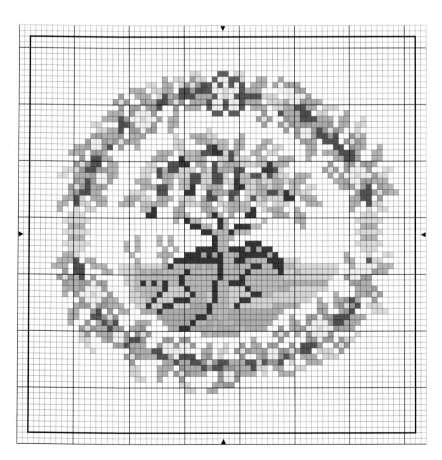

Fig 8.5 **Chart for centre of Emblem table carpet**

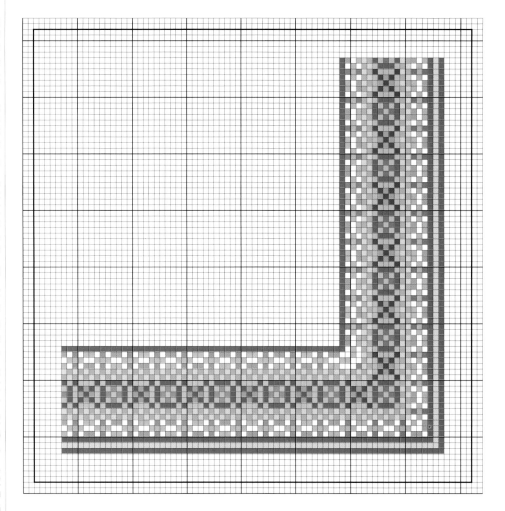

Fig 8.6 **Chart for border of Emblem table carpet**

Border Table Carpet

Some of the table carpets of the sixteenth and seventeenth centuries were made of velvet with a border of applied embroidery or braided decoration. This project is intended to simulate this by using a coloured evenweave fabric and a counted threadwork border.

Border Table Carpet

Materials

Evenweave fabric, coloured or dyed (32 count):

  200 x 160mm (8 x 6¼in),

  or 80mm (3in) larger overall than the size of the table top

Stranded cotton in black

Stranded metallic thread in gold

Tacking cotton

Tapestry needle: No. 26

Size

132 x 91mm (5¼ x 3½in), or as desired

Fig 8.7 **Border table carpet**

Working method

1 Prepare as step 1 for the Landscape carpet.

2 Mount the fabric in a small rectangular frame (*see* page 137).

3 Refer to chart (*see* Fig 8.8) and, using one thread and backstitch throughout, begin the border in the centre of one long side.

4 Work towards and turn the corner when the desired size is achieved.

5 When the embroidery is complete, remove the fabric from the frame.

6 Finish the edges as directed on page 114.

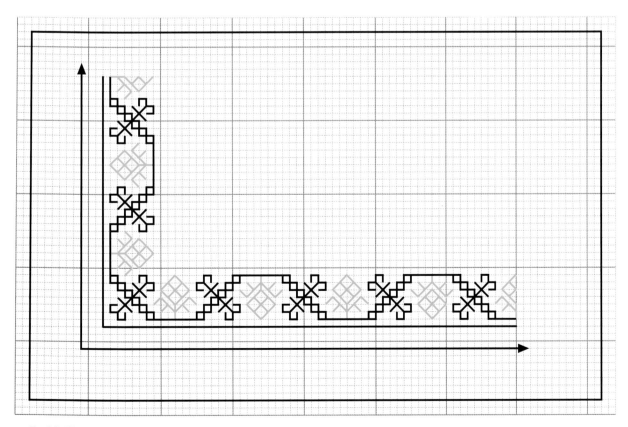

Fig 8.8 **Chart for Border table carpet**

Completing the edges of a table carpet

1 Trim the excess turning to about 6mm (¼in).

2 Remove a little fabric diagonally from each corner (*see* Fig 8.9) and turn under.

3 Turn under the edge of each side and use one of the following methods.

4 Either, from the right side, using sewing cotton, stitch through the hem with a small running stitch. If you stitch along a row of holes in the fabric, the running stitch should disappear between the embroidery.

Or, using fabric glue very sparingly, secure the hem with glue. When dry, lightly press the hem with a warm iron to give a sharper crease to the edge.

Fitting a carpet on to a table

1 Cut a piece of very lightweight iron-on interlining to fit on the reverse of the carpet between the hem turnings: i.e. a little smaller than the actual carpet. Press into place with an iron.

2 Dilute some PVA glue; 1 part glue to 4 of water.

3 Spread the diluted glue on to the ironed-on interlining, sufficient to wet the back but not soak the carpet.

4 Completely cover the table with cling film.

5 Mould the table carpet into position on the table top and leave to dry completely. The glue will stiffen the carpet.

6 When dry, the carpet can be eased gently from the table. Remove the cling film and replace the table carpet on the table.

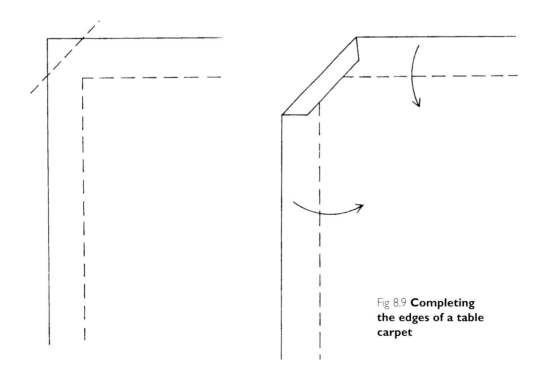

Fig 8.9 **Completing the edges of a table carpet**

Fig 8.10 **Music Makers wall hanging**

Wall Hangings

During the sixteenth and seventeenth centuries it was fashionable to hang the walls with embroidered hangings and woven tapestries to enhance the building and to provide some degree of warmth. Later in the seventeenth century, the fashion was for wood panelling in the main rooms. To avoid covering the costly panelling, small pictures became popular instead of large hangings.

Most of the very large embroidered hangings would have been produced in workshops, as of course, were the woven tapestries. However, some hangings were worked in the domestic environment. This was facilitated by working small pieces and applying them to a velvet or silk ground.

Any of the table carpet projects can be used as wall hangings.

Music Makers Wall Hanging

The inspiration of this project came from an embroidered bed valance from the late sixteenth century. Although the original tells the story of Jephthah, the ladies are dressed in sumptuous Elizabethan dress, and shown dancing through a landscape playing percussion instruments.

Working method

1 Using tacking thread, mark the size of the hanging on the linen. Do this by measuring to find an initial approximate size. Then mark the vertical and horizontal centres.

2 Mount the fabric in a small rectangular frame (*see* page 137).

3 The four sections of the chart (*see* Fig 8.10) fit together without any spaces in between. Begin at one of the lower outside corners, as the work progresses it is easy to position the various figures.

4 Use one thread of stranded cotton and tent stitch throughout.

5 When the embroidery is complete, remove

Music Makers Wall Hanging

Materials

Evenweave linen (35 count): 250 x 230mm (10 x 9in)
Stranded cotton as listed in colour key
Tacking cotton
Tapestry needle: No. 26 or 28
Dark green fabric or ribbon for loops (*see* below)

Size

165 x 130mm (6½ x 5⅛in)

the fabric from the frame. and finish the edges as for the table carpets (*see* page 114).

6 Add the hanging loops using one of the following alternatives:

a Either cut a strip of dark green fabric 20mm (¾in) wide and 150mm (6in) long. Fold it down the length turning 6mm (¼in) over, press with an iron. Fold the remaining side over 6mm (¼in) and secure with a little PVA fabric glue. Cut into six equal pieces, fold in half and stitch or glue to the top of the hanging on the reverse (*see* Fig 8.11).

b Or, use 6mm (¼in) ribbon and cut into six pieces and attach as above.

Fig 8.11 **Making the hanging loops for a wall hanging**

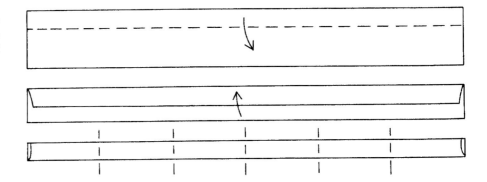

Music Makers Wall Hanging

		Skeins	DMC	Anchor	Madeira
	Navy blue	I	823	152	1008
	Dark blue	I	820	134	0904
	Mid blue	I	799	145	0910
	Light blue	I	800	159	1002
	Dark brown	I	898	360	2006
	Mid brown	I	433	371	2008
	Light brown	I	435	1046	2010
	Dark gold	I	680	907	2210
	Yellow	I	444	297	0105
	Pale yellow	I	744	301	0110
	Dark red	I	815	43	0512
	Red	I	321	47	0510
	Dark peach	I	352	9	0303
	Mid peach	I	353	868	0304
	Light peach	I	754	1012	0305
	Flesh	I	951	880	2308
	White	I	Blanc	White	White
	Dark green	I	500	879	1705
	Mid green	I	502	876	1703
	Light green	I	504	1042	1701
	Bright green	I	906	256	1410

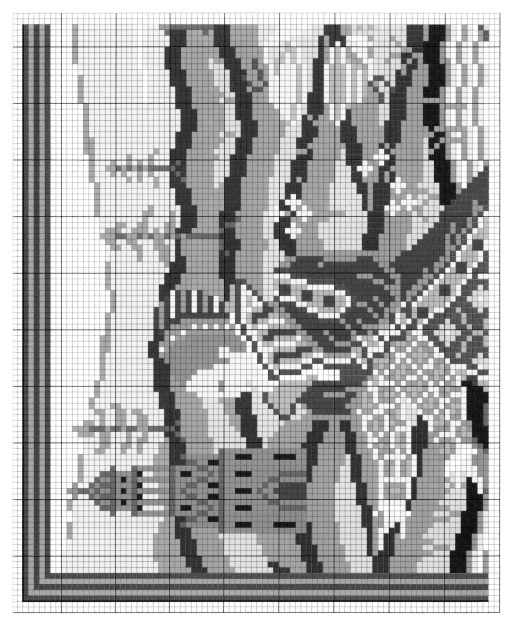

Fig 8.12A **Chart for Music Makers wall hanging**

Fig 8.12B **Chart for Music Makers wall hanging**

Fig 8.12C **Chart for Music Makers wall hanging**

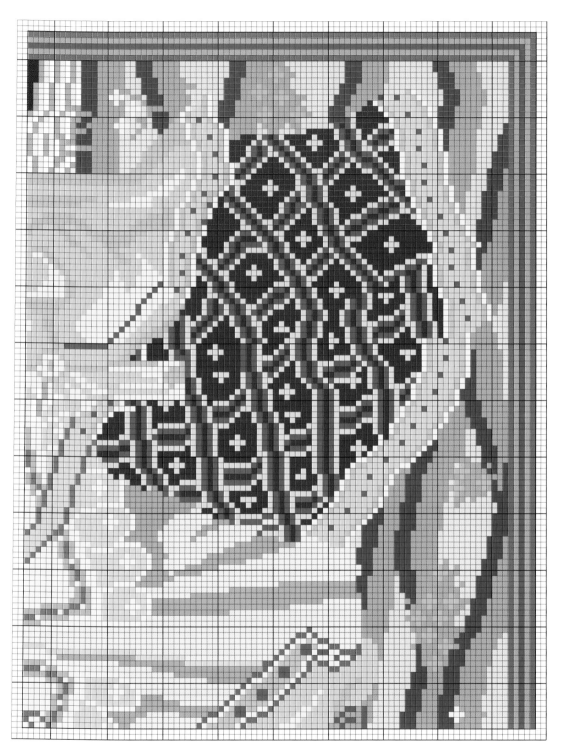

Fig 8.12D **Chart for Music Makers wall hanging**

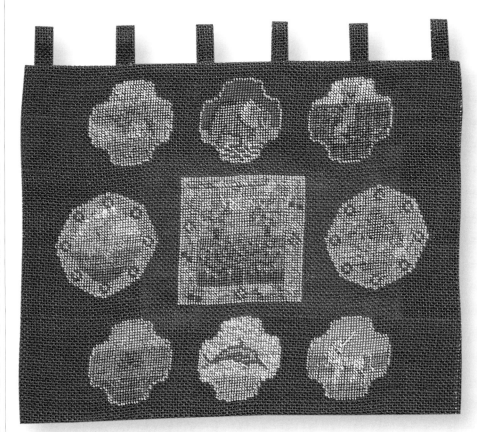

Fig 8.13 **Oxburgh wall hanging**

Oxburgh Wall Hanging

This project (*see* Fig 8.13) has the same origin as the bed shown in Fig 2.3 (*see* page 12), and uses the same charts (*see* Figs 2.5, 2.6 and 2.7).

The individual motifs can be selected and placed as desired, and should be symmetrical so as to look balanced. Place the largest in the centre and the remaining motifs arranged around it.

Oxburgh Wall Hanging

Materials

Evenweave linen (32 count): 220 x 200mm (8¾ x 8in), or 75mm (3in) larger overall than the desired size

Stranded cotton as listed in colour key (*see* page 14)

Tacking cotton

Tapestry needle: No. 26

Size

130 x 100mm (5⅛ x 4in), or as desired

Working method

1 Using tacking thread, mark the size of the wall hanging on the linen. Do this by measuring to find an initial approximate size. Then mark the vertical and horizontal centres.

2 Mount the fabric in a small rectangular frame (*see* page 137).

3 Using one strand of stranded cotton and tent stitch throughout, work the centre motif first and then use this to position the other motifs. Leave six or eight threads between the motifs.

4 Remove the fabric from the frame and finish the edges as for the table carpets (*see* page 114).

5 Add the hanging loops as directed for the Music Makers hanging (*see* page 116).

Slips Wall Hanging

This little wall hanging is based on the charts for the slips bed (*see* Fig 2.8, page 17). It can be made to any size required simply by repeating the motifs (*see* Fig 2.11). The hanging shown in Fig 8.14 is the size quoted below.

Working methods are basically the same as the Oxburgh hanging above. However, begin with the centre row of motifs and then work to each side until the size required is reached.

Make up as for the Music Makers hanging (*see* page 116).

Slips Wall Hanging

Materials
As for Oxburgh hanging, left (*see* page 122).

Size
108 x 82mm (4¼ x 3¼in)

Fig 8.14 **Slips wall hanging**

Millefleurs 'Tapestry'

The charts given for the Millefleurs three-fold screen (*see* Fig 6.4, pages 84–5) can be used for a wall hanging.

Simply work as for the screen without leaving any space between the three panels.

Make up as for the Music Makers hanging (*see* page 116).

Millefleurs 'Tapestry'

Materials
As for screen, without the wood (*see* page 83)

Size
Approximately 126 x 120mm (5 x 4¾in)

9 Decorative items

During the sixteenth and seventeenth centuries, embroidered items were many and various. Most pieces of furniture had a decorated cover; some mirrors had elaborate embroidered frames; precious books had rich covers with cushions to protect their surfaces. Ladies would carry small, highly decorated bags with matching tiny pin cushions. They would also have had pin cushions of various sizes in their rooms as most of their clothing was in separate pieces which were pinned together.

Fig 9.1 **Mirror frame**

Mirror Frame

The design for this project is based on the stumpwork mirror frames of the mid-seventeenth century. The originals would have been in raised stitchery on a satin ground. However, this project is presented as counted thread to ease the method of working.

Mirror Frame

Materials

Evenweave linen (40 count): 120 x 100mm (4¾ x 4in)

Stranded cotton as listed in colour key

Tacking cotton

Tapestry needle: No. 28

Mounting card: 2mm (⅒in) thick, 120 x 100mm (4¾ x 4in)

PVA glue

Miniature picture-frame moulding: 30cm (12in)

Small piece mirror effect card

Size

57mm x 50mm (2¼ x 2in)

Working method

1 Mark the size of the Mirror frame on the fabric with tacking stitches.

2 Mount the fabric in a card frame or small rectangular frame.

3 Using one strand of stranded cotton and tent stitch throughout, refer to the chart (*see* Fig 9.2), and begin the embroidery at one of the lower corners. As each motif is worked it will provide a reference for the placement of the next one.

4 When the embroidery is complete, remove the fabric from the frame, and make up as follows.

Fig 9.2 **Chart for the Mirror frame**

Mirror Frame

		Skeins	DMC	Anchor	Madeira
	Dark green	1	937	268	1504
	Mid green	1	906	256	1410
	Light green	1	472	264	1414
	Dark blue	1	820	134	0904
	Light blue	1	827	9159	1014
	Dark brown	1	839	1050	1913
	Light brown	1	612	888	2108
	Red	1	321	47	0510
	Pink	1	776	24	0607
	Flesh	1	543	933	1909
	Silver	1	Metallic	Metallic	Metallic
	Gold	1	Metallic	Metallic	Metallic
	White	1	Blanc	White	White

Mounting and framing the mirror

1 Make the frame for the outside edge from the miniature picture-frame moulding using the directions given for pictures and samplers (*see* Fig 7.13, page 104).

2 Prepare the 'window' in the embroidered fabric for the mirror card (*see* Fig 9.3A). Carefully cut the fabric as shown and fold each side through to the reverse. Using PVA fabric glue *very sparingly*, secure each flap behind the embroidery. Make sure the embroidery is square at all times by trying the frame over it. Leave to dry completely.

3 Glue the small piece of mirror card in the centre of the mounting card (*see* Fig 9.3B).

4 Lightly glue the area of card surrounding the 'mirror', and press the embroidery in place, checking that it is square with the frame.

5 Glue the frame over the embroidery and allow to dry completely.

6 Finally, with a sharp craft knife, cut away the excess card and fabric from around the edges.

Fig 9.3A **Mounting the Mirror frame**

Fig 9.3B **Mounting the Mirror frame**

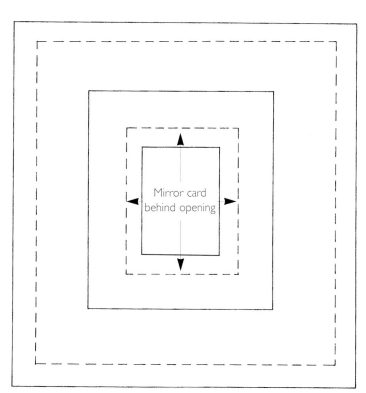

Fig 9.4 **Two Book covers and book cushions (actual size)**

Book Covers and Cushions

These items were often embroidered and given as precious gifts. Many have survived and can be seen in museums and national libraries. They vary greatly in size from 75 x 100mm (3 x 4in) to 200 x 130mm (8 x 5in).

The cushions, which are to protect books from a hard or rough surface when being used, are quite flat.

Working method

1 Mount both pieces of fabric in a card frame or small rectangular frame.

2 Using one strand of stranded cotton and tent stitch throughout, refer to the charts (*see* Fig 9.5 or Fig 9.6) and begin with the outside row of stitches. This gives you the outline.

3 Continue with the remaining design.

4 When the embroidery is complete, remove the fabric from the frame, and make up as instructed on page 130.

Book Covers and Cushions

Materials

For book cover: evenweave linen (40 count): 100mm (4in) square

For cushion: evenweave linen (35 count): 100mm (4in) square

Stranded cotton as listed in colour key

Tapestry needle: No. 28

PVA fabric glue

Small amount of wadding

Stripwood: 3mm (⅛in) thick x 25mm (1in) square

Size

Book cover: 23 x 14mm (⅞in x ⁹⁄₁₆in)

Book cushion: 27 x 18mm (1¹⁄₁₆in x ¾in)

Red Book Cover and Cushion

		Skeins	DMC	Anchor	Madeira
	Gold	I	Metallic	Metallic	Metallic
	Red	I	816	1005	0512

Blue Book Cover and Cushion

		Skeins	DMC	Anchor	Madeira
	Red	I	321	47	0510
	Dark red	I	816	1005	0512
	Gold	I	Metallic	Metallic	Metallic
	Green	I	906	256	1410
	Blue	I	799	145	0910

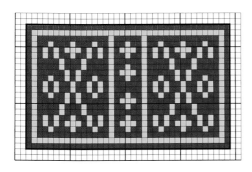

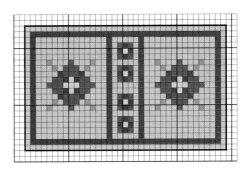

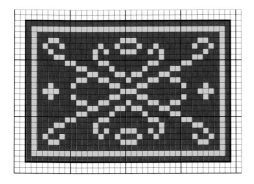

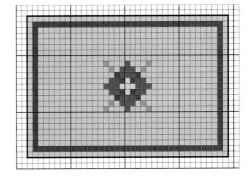

Fig 9.5 **Chart for the red Book cover and cushion**

Fig 9.6 **Chart for the blue Book cover and cushion**

Making up and mounting the book cover

1 Trim the turnings on the two long sides to 3mm (⅛in). Using the PVA fabric glue very sparingly, turn the two edges under and secure (*see* Fig 9.7A). Allow to dry.

2 Trim the two short sides to 6mm (¼in) and glue under as above (*see* Fig 9.7B).

3 Cut the stripwood into a piece 12 x 8mm (⁷⁄₁₆ x ⁵⁄₁₆in)and shape gently with sandpaper as shown in Fig 9.7C.

4 Paint the three edges gold if desired, but not the spine.

5 Place a little glue on the spine and fold the book cover in position around the wood block. Place a small weight on the covered book until the glue is dry.

Making up the cushion

Refer to the instructions in Figs 4.25 and 4.26 (*see* page 67). However, remember not to insert much filling, as the book cushion needs to be fairly flat so that the book rests on it.

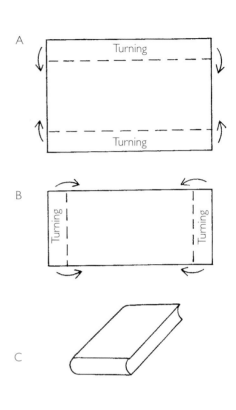

Fig 9.7 **Making up the Book covers**

Pin Cushions

Fig 9.8 **Pin cushions (actual size)**

Pin cushions were a very necessary item for a lady, who would have had several in different sizes, including a tiny one to fit in her bag. Costume was assembled from various items: the petticoat, seen at the front between a divided skirt; a bodice laced at the front, covered with a stomacher; and sleeves.

Pins varied from base metal to gold and silver. Larger versions of the pin cushions were used to pin jewellery on when it was not in use.

The projects given here (*see* Fig 9.8) are typical in design showing the scrolling stem and a heraldic device. Both projects are worked in exactly the same way and other counts of fabric can be used to give different sizes.

Working method

1 Mount the fabric in a card frame.

2 Refer to the chart (*see* Fig 9.9) and, using

Pin Cushions

Materials

Evenweave linen (40 count): 50mm (2in) square

Stranded cotton as listed in colour key

Small amount of wadding for filling

Size

20 x 13mm (¾ x ½in)

one strand of stranded cotton and tent stitch throughout, work the embroidery.

3 When complete, remove the fabric from the frame and make up as for the book cushions, keeping the filling to a minimum.

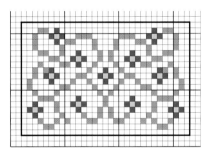

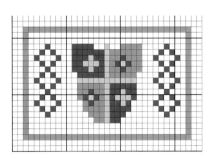

Fig 9.9 **Charts for the Pin cushions**

Pin Cushions

		Skeins	DMC	Anchor	Madeira
	Green	I	906	256	1410
	Red	I	321	47	0510
	Yellow	I	444	297	0105

Fig 9.10 **Lady's bag (actual size)**

Lady's Bag

Ladies would carry small highly decorated bags with them. These were often made and given as gifts. They would be finished with beautiful cords and ornate tassels. The bags were generally between 115mm (4½in) and 150mm (6in) square and often included a tiny pin cushion to match.

Working method

1 Mount the fabric in a card frame or small rectangular frame.

2 Using one thread of stranded or metallic and tent stitch throughout, begin with the outside row of stitches. This will give the size of the bag (*see* Fig 9.11).

3 Continue with the rest of the design.

4 When the embroidery is complete, remove the fabric from the frame, and make up as follows.

Lady's Bag

Materials

Evenweave linen (40 count): 100mm (4in) square

Stranded and metallic threads listed in colour key

Tapestry needle: No 28

PVA fabric glue

Size

12mm (½in) square

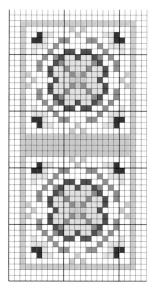

Fig 9.11 **Chart for the Lady's bag**

Lady's Bag		Skeins	DMC	Anchor	Madeira
	Gold	I	Metallic	Metallic	Metallic
	Green	I	906	256	1410
	Dark blue	I	820	134	0904
	Light blue	I	827	9159	1014
	Red	I	321	47	0510
	Pink	I	776	24	0607

Making up a bag

1 Trim the excess fabric from all four sides to 3mm (⅛in) and turn under. Secure with a tiny amount of PVA fabric glue (*see* Fig 9.12A).

2 Fold the bag in half and stitch the two sides together (*see* Fig 9.12B).

3 Either, twist together one strand of each thread used to make a cord, or, use a slightly thicker metallic thread.

4 Begin at the lower corner of the bag and stitch the 'cord' to the side of the bag, leaving a length for a strap and then stitch down the remaining side of the bag (*see* Fig 9.12C).

5 Leave the ends of the cord at both the lower corner and trim to form tassels.

A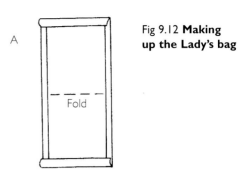

Fold

Fig 9.12 Making up the Lady's bag

B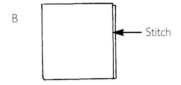

Stitch

C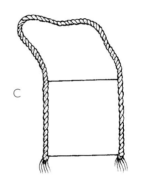

10 Working to 1/24 scale

Most of the projects in this book could be adapted to 1/24 scale. The working methods and general instructions remain the same for both scales.

Given that most of the items can, in full scale, vary in size considerably, it is not necessary that a 1/24-scale version should be exactly half the size of a 1/12 scale item. For example, samplers can be very small or quite large. A small 1/12 version worked on finer fabric could represent a large sampler in 1/24 scale.

Scaling down counted thread projects

Projects based on canvas or evenweave linen can be reduced in size by using a different count fabric, as suggested below. Use one strand of stranded cotton, or substitute machine-embroidery threads.

Item	1/12 scale	1/24 scale
Table carpets	32, 35, 40 evenweave	80–120 silk gauze
Cushions	22, 24 canvas	40 evenweave
	35 evenweave	80–120 silk gauze
Chair covers	35 evenweave	80–120 silk gauze
Footstools	35, 40 evenweave	80–120 silk gauze
Pictures	35, 40 evenweave	80–120 silk gauze
Wall hangings	32, 35 evenweave	80–120 silk gauze
Samplers	32, 35, 40 evenweave	80–120 silk gauze
Screens	35, 40 evenweave	80–120 silk gauze
Bed hangings, covers	32, 35 evenweave	40 evenweave or
		80–120 silk gauze
Small items	35, 40 evenweave	80–120 silk gauze

Scaling down projects worked on other fabrics

Generally, projects would be worked on the same lightweight silk and cotton fabrics recommended for 1/12 scale.

Patterns and designs can be reduced to half size on a photocopier.

Use one strand of stranded cotton or machine-embroidery threads.

Bed hanging and cover patterns can be reduced as suggested above.

The crewelwork patterns and designs for the cushions, chair covers, footstools, wall hangings and screens are easily reduced to half size.

11 Materials and working methods

Fabrics

Canvas

Canvas is available in various counts – the number of threads to 25mm (1in). The higher the number of threads, the finer the canvas.

Single-thread canvas, also known as mono canvas, is used for the projects in this book. This can be purchased in white, pale yellow or 'antique' brown.

Interlock canvas is white, with a twisted weave in one direction. It is more pliable than the normal weave. Interlock canvas can be cut to a shape without fraying.

Coin net is a cotton canvas with a 24 count.

Evenweaves

Evenweaves can be woven from linen, cotton or, less commonly, rayon. They are also sold in various counts.

Linen is the easiest fabric to work on as the linen threads are finer, which means the holes are larger by comparison.

Cotton evenweaves appear to be more closely woven because the cotton threads are thicker than linen and slightly fluffy, making the hole seem smaller.

Hardanger and Aida fabrics have threads which are woven in

blocks, forming 'squares'. Generally, these fabrics are too coarse for miniature work.

Silk

Habutai silk is a white silk fabric with a flat surface. It can be obtained in various weights, the lightest being ideal for miniature work.

Cotton

Lawn is a lightweight, smooth fabric which can be bought either plain or patterned. It is ideal for miniature projects.

Voile is lighter in weight than lawn and has a more open weave. Muslin is even more loosely woven than lawn or voile.

Wadding

Waddings come in various weights and thicknesses. Some are very fluffy and these are often too thick for miniature work. Others are more like a soft interlining and are more suitable for working to a miniature scale.

Domette is a light, knitted interlining with a brushed surface.

Felt, being a soft, compacted fabric, can be used effectively as a padding.

Embroidery frames

Most of the projects in this book will benefit from being worked in an embroidery frame. When working on canvas and evenweave fabrics, the frame will help to reduce distortion. It is also easier to be precise with the stitching when the fabric is stabilized in a frame.

There are various types of frame: slate frames, stretchers, card mounts and tambour (round) frames. Each requires a different method of preparation.

Slate frames

Slate frames are rectangular-shaped and consist of two sides with circular notches, into which the two rounded sides with webbing are fixed. Wing nuts at each corner tension the material, which can be adjusted by rolling the rounded sides. Fig 11.1 shows how to mount the fabric.

Fig 11.1 **Using a slate frame**

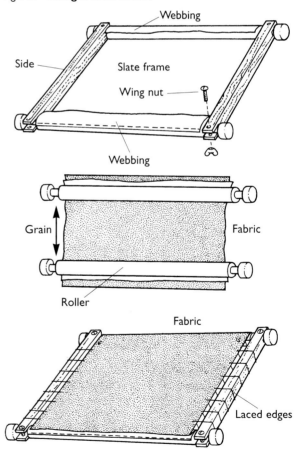

137

Dismantle the frame and lay the two webbing strips face down on two opposite sides of the fabric. Make sure the fabric is on the straight grain.

Stitch through the fabric and webbing using backstitch with a strong thread. Fasten on and off securely.

Locate the rounded sides in the notches in the square sides, and roll until the fabric is tensioned. Tighten the wing nuts.

Lace the fabric to the remaining two square sides with a strong thread to tension the fabric in both directions.

Stretchers

A simpler form of frame can be made by using artist stretchers, which are available in many sizes. The sides are purchased in pairs of the desired length, with tongue and groove ends which are simply pushed together.

It is also possible to buy a smaller version of these, usually as an assorted pack, made especially for embroiderers. These are very useful for working small projects (*see* Fig 11.2).

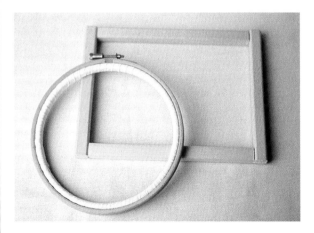

Fig 11.2 **A small stretcher and a round frame**

Fig 11.3 **Using a stretcher**

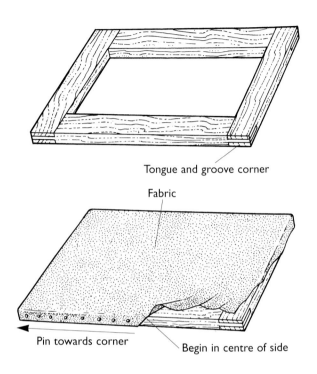

Tongue and groove corner

Fabric

Pin towards corner

Begin in centre of side

Alternatively, a homemade version can be made using angle brackets to hold the corners. Assemble the stretcher by pushing the corners together, making sure the frame is square at the corners. Fig 11.3 shows how to mount the fabric.

Using drawing pins or thumbtacks, pin the fabric along one of the longer sides, stretching the fabric slightly.

Then pin the opposite side, stretching the fabric slightly and making sure the grain of the fabric is straight across the centre.

Pin the remaining two sides in the same way, making sure that the grain of the fabric is straight at all times.

Card mounts

It is possible to cut a mount from sturdy card for very small pieces of fabric.

Choose a piece of card at least 10cm (4in) larger, in both directions than the piece of embroidery to be worked.

Mark and cut a window in the centre, leaving a border of 40mm (1½in) around the edges (*see* Fig 11.4).

On the reverse side of the card, spread a line of PVA glue around the centre opening. Allow to dry completely (*see* Fig 11.5).

Place the fabric over the opening, with the right side showing through to the right side of the card, and press around the opening with a warm iron. This will dry mount the fabric into the opening, ready for embroidery.

Fig 11.4 **Making a card frame for small pieces of fabric.**

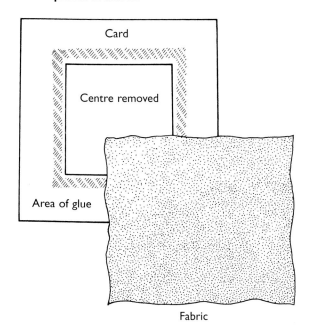

Fig 11.5 **Card mounts showing the reverse and the mount in use.**

Note: When mounting canvas in this way, it is necessary to place the canvas in position while the PVA glue is still wet, as canvas does not dry mount well. It is also advisable to be rather more generous with the glue when mounting canvas as opposed to other fabrics.

Tambour or round frames

These frames are made in wood or plastic. The wooden ones are best as the fabric does not slip, especially if the inner ring is covered with binding or strips of fabric (*see* Figs 11.6 and 11.2).

To mount the embroidery fabric, lay the inner ring down on a surface. Position the fabric over the inner ring. Push the outer ring onto the inner ring, pulling the fabric taut, and tighten the tensioning screw.

Fig 11.6 **A tambour or round frame**

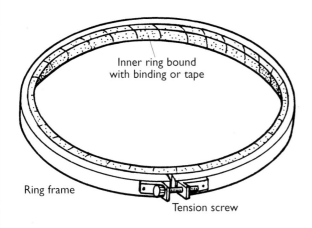

Inner ring bound
with binding or tape

Ring frame

Tension screw

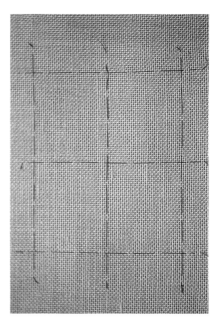

Fig 11.7 **Marking outlines and centres
with tacking thread**

Spring frames

If you choose to embroider by machine, a spring frame can be used which fits under the foot of the machine more easily. This is a metal sprung ring which fits into a plastic outer ring.

When fitting fabric for machine embroidery, lay the outer ring on a surface. Position the fabric over the outer ring. Push the inner ring into the outer ring, pulling the fabric taut. The inner spring frame will hold the fabric taut while you stitch.

Beginning to stitch

Most of the projects require the fabric to be marked with small tacking stitches to show the outer edges and the vertical and horizontal centres.

On canvas and evenweave fabrics this can be done easily by following the weave of the fabric (*see* Fig 11.7). On other fabrics this can be achieved by cutting out a paper pattern as a

guide, or by using the trace and tack method described in Chapter 12 (*see* page 142).

Using a chart

On most of the charts each square is solid colour. This indicates one individual stitch, usually tent or cross stitch as stated in the working instructions.

Some of the sampler charts show the use of both solid squares and lines within or on the edge of a square. Each line indicates the position of a small straight stitch, over one thread, in the direction of the line on the chart.

Working on canvas and evenweave

To begin, make a knot in the end of the embroidery thread and take the thread through

Fig 11.8 **Beginning with a knot
(front and reverse shown)**

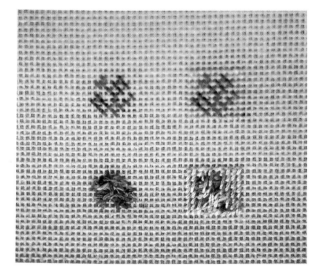

Fig 11.9 **Stitching on canvas
(front and reverse shown)**

the canvas or evenweave, from the front, about 15mm (½in) from where the first stitch is to be made. Bring the thread back through the canvas or evenweave at the position of the first stitch.

Proceed with the stitching, which will eventually cover the length of thread on the back between the knot and the first stitch. The knot on the front of the work can then be cut away (*see* Fig 11.8).

Many charts require stitches to be spaced about. Using the colour required, work the stitches as indicated on the chart, taking the thread across the back of the canvas as necessary. When an area of design has been worked, the background can be filled in, covering all the threads on the back (*see* Fig 11.9).

12
Methods of transferring designs

Dressmakers' carbon

This is a form of carbon paper used by dressmakers to outline patterns. The carbon comes in blue, red, white and yellow and washes out after use.

The carbon is placed face down onto the fabric with the design placed on top. The lines of the design can then be traced onto the fabric. I find that a worn-out biro gives a good line as it is harder than a pencil.

Care should be taken not to smudge the carbon by pressing on it with your fingers.

Trace and tack

This is a good method for larger, simple designs, especially for putting the basic outline of a shape onto the fabric.

Trace the outline onto tissue paper. Then lay the tissue paper onto the fabric and stitch through the lines with a large running stitch and tacking cotton. Fasten on and off securely. Carefully tear off the tissue paper, leaving the stitches to mark the shape.

Tracing through fabric

Some fabrics are fine enough to see through when laid on top of a design. This is usually possible if the design has been drawn in black ink or is on a printed page.

Lay the fabric over the design and, with a fabric transfer pencil or soluble pen (*see* below), trace the lines of the design onto the fabric.

Embroidery transfer pencils

The purpose of a transfer pencil is literally to create a transfer, i.e. to trace a design onto paper which can then be ironed off onto fabric. The pencil line will wash out after use.

These pencils can also be used directly onto the fabric. Always have a very sharp point as this gives a fine line which will be hidden by the stitchery and may not need to be washed out on completion of the work.

Remember that if the iron-off method is used, the design will be reversed.

Soluble pens

Water-soluble and air-soluble pens are widely used by embroiderers. They are similar to a felt-tip pen, usually giving a pink or blue line.

The water-soluble ink can be removed with a damp cotton bud after use, or by washing the completed item if that is feasible. The air-soluble pens should only be used for very short-term pieces, as the ink disappears within a few hours.

Transfer with photocopies

A design can be photocopied onto paper and the resulting copy can then be ironed off onto fabric. This method works better on fabrics of natural fibres, i.e. cotton or silk. Some synthetics are resistant, but it is always worth trying.

This method reverses the design, but it has the advantage of being very quick and simple.

A colour photocopy can be made directly onto fabric or canvas. This can be used to produce 'tapestries' or wall hangings, etc. Fine calico is a good base to use.

For designs embroidered in counted thread, evenweave or canvas is required. Use the colour copy as a guide, placing the correctly coloured stitches directly over it.

The designs can usually be enlarged or reduced with considerable precision, so it is possible to recreate the exact scale.

Once the photocopy is on the fabric, the embroidery can be worked as if on a printed canvas, in tent or cross stitch.

13 Bonding methods and colouring techniques

Bonding methods

Bond-a-web

Bond-a-web is a brand name for a web of adhesive which is supported by non-stick paper. It can be used to bond two fabrics together, or to bond fabric to paper or card.

The Bond-a-web is placed onto the reverse side of the fabric with the adhesive next to the fabric, i.e. paper side uppermost. An iron is used to bond the adhesive, set to the correct heat for the fabric.

Once the Bond-a-web and the fabric have bonded, the paper can be removed from the back of the Bond-a-web. The fabric can then be turned over and bonded in the same way to another surface.

It is a good idea to have a piece of non-stick baking paper on the ironing surface, and between the iron and the piece being bonded, to protect the work surface and iron.

Bonding powder

This is a powdered form of Bond-a-web adhesive which is used by embroiderers when small or scattered areas are to be bonded for creative effects.

The powder is sprinkled over the surface and small fragments of thread or fabric are then added. A sheet of non-stick paper is placed over the whole surface and pressed with an iron.

Bonded interlinings

There are several brands of bonded interlining available. Some are woven and some, like Vilene, are a fused fabric.

The interlining has a web of adhesive on one side which can be used to stiffen fabric or to prevent fabric fraying.

The interlinings come in various weights, the lightest being ultra-light and the heaviest pelmet weight. An iron is used to bond the lining to the fabric; it should be set to the correct heat for the fabric being used.

Adhesives

The only safe adhesive to use with fabric is one with a PVA base. This is basically a plastic glue which, when dry, will not change with time. Other glues with rubber or solvent bases are best avoided.

PVA adhesives come in various strengths. Wood glue is very strong; fabric glue is more dilute. These glues can be diluted further with water. Wood glue is hard when dry, fabric glue remains pliable.

The wood glue can be used for dry mounting. A thin layer of glue is applied to a card, wood or paper surface and left to dry completely. The fabric can then be bonded with an iron to the dry area of glue. If the placement is not initially correct, apply the iron again and peel off the fabric.

Fabric dyes and paints

There are many different types of fabric paint and dye available. Some are for particular fabrics, e.g. silk dyes for silk, special dyes for natural fibres, others for synthetics. If the correct type is used and the individual manufacturer's instructions are followed for use and fixing, the resulting fabric should be washable. If the item is never going to be washed, as with most miniature pieces, any dyes or paints can be used on any fabric, even artists' watercolours.

Some fabrics, for example linen, which have a high level of natural oils or dressing may require more than one application of colour.

When colouring a small area, the dye or paint is best applied with a brush rather than immersing the fabric. Place the fabric in a frame so that it is taut and smooth. Apply the dye or paint with a small brush. Leave to dry in the frame on a level surface so that the dye dries evenly. A completed piece of work can be 'antiqued' by painting on a solution of cold black tea. Test on a spare piece of fabric first to see how it turns out.

Painting freehand

If you are unable to find a suitable fabric, or wish to reproduce some of the projects as a painted surface, this can be achieved by painting directly onto fabric.

Fabric paints are available which are thicker in consistency than those which are water based. These paints can be applied to fabric without the paint bleeding because the paint stays on the surface of the fabric. For fine details use a size 0 or 00 pointed paintbrush. When the completed piece is ironed, the colours will be fast and washable.

Watercolour and acrylic paints can also be used. As these are water based, the amount of paint loaded onto the brush must be carefully considered. The brush needs to be wet enough to take up the paint, but not so wet that the fabric absorbs any water. This is sometimes called 'dry brush technique'. It works best on a fine, smooth fabric such as cotton or silk and, although colourfast to light will not be washable.

Fabric transfer paints

There are several brands of fabric transfer paint available, but all will have the word 'transfer' somewhere on the label. They are made for use on synthetic fabrics, on which they give the brightest colours. When used on natural fibres the colours are softer.

Transfer paints and dyes are painted onto paper and then ironed off onto fabric. Remember that this will reverse the design.

There is sometimes a considerable difference in the colours when they have been ironed off onto the fabric. A sample strip should be made first to see the colour before using on the actual piece.

A photocopy of the design can be used. Colour this with the transfer paints and iron off, with the iron set at the correct heat for the fabric.

Alternatively, a tracing onto detail paper can be used. Tracing paper itself is not successful. Detail paper, sometimes marketed as 'marker pads', is a white, opaque paper that is see-through when placed over a design.

When ironing off the transfer, move the iron gently and smoothly so that the paper remains in the same place. It may take several minutes for the colour to transfer onto some fabrics. Place a piece of paper under the fabric to protect the working surface.

14 Finishing methods

Making tassels

The tassel should initially be made longer than required as it is then easier to handle.

Working method

1 Cut a piece of stiff card into a rectangle 100 x 60mm (4 x 2⅜in), then cut a piece from the centre 50 x 30mm (2 x 1¹⁄₁₆in). Mark the centre line and cut a small notch in one end of the card to secure the threads (*see* Fig 14.1A).

2 Wind the thread around the card until the required thickness of tassel is achieved. Do not make the tassel too thick, as it will look out of scale (*see* Fig 14.1B).

3 Bind the middle 10–15mm (⅜–½in) of the tassel using the centre mark as a guide. Cut the threads at each end of the card (*see* Fig 14.1C).

4 Bend the tassel in half and bind the head to form a loop. Finally, trim the ends of the threads to the required length: probably 10–15mm (⅜–½in) (*see* Fig 14.1D).

Fig 14.1 **The stages in making a tassel**

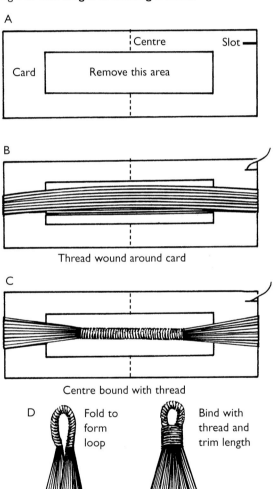

A

Card — Centre — Slot

Remove this area

B

Thread wound around card

C

Centre bound with thread

D Fold to form loop

Bind with thread and trim length

Making fringes

Here are two methods of making miniature fringes. The first is based on a strip of fabric, the second is a knotted edging.

Working method: fabric fringes

Almost any fine fabric can be used, e.g. silk, cotton and linen.

1 Cut a strip of fabric about 50mm (2in) wide and at least 100mm (4in) longer than the required length of fringed edging.

2 Work two rows of straight machine stitching, close together, down the length of the strip of fabric and along the straight grain. The example in Fig 14.2. has been stitched in a contrasting thread for clarity.

3 Trim away the excess fabric along the upper edge, close to the stitching.

4 Set the machine to a zigzag stitch and a short stitch length. Machine along the strip over the straight stitching, enclosing the top edge. A perle cotton or fine braid can be incorporated at this stage if desired.

5 Trim the lower edge of the fabric to the required width of the fringe.

6 Fray the fabric back to the machine stitching, removing one thread at a time.

7 Stitch or glue the fringe into position on the item to be decorated.

Working method: knotted fringes

1 Turn under the edge of the fabric or canvas.

2 Cut the thread or cord into lengths. A manageable length is about 100mm (4in).

3 Fold these lengths in half and pull them through the edge of the hem with a fine crochet hook to form a loop (*see* Fig 14.3).

4 Slip the two ends of the thread down through the loop and pull them firmly to tighten the knot.

5 Trim the threads to the desired length when the whole row of knots has been completed.

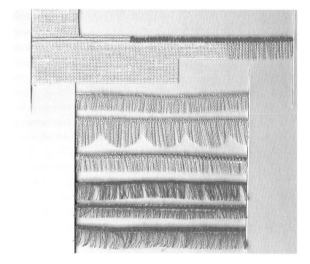

Fig 14.2 **Making a fabric fringe.**

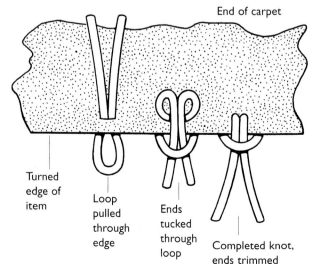

Fig 14.3 **Making a knotted fringe.**

End of carpet

Turned edge of item

Loop pulled through edge

Ends tucked through loop

Completed knot, ends trimmed

Blocking embroidery

Counted-thread embroidery on linen or canvas often distorts with the tension of the stitches. The use of a frame will help to prevent this, but you may need to block the finished embroidery back into shape.

Before blocking, make sure all threads used are colourfast, and test any painted backgrounds to make sure the dyes are fixed. Moisten a small corner and blot with tissue to see if any colour transfers to the tissue.

Blocking

Materials

Pinboard or similar, soft enough to take drawing pins or thumbtacks
Paper
Transparent plastic sheeting
Drawing pins or thumbtacks
Waterproof pen

Working method

1 Draw a rectangle on a sheet of paper using the waterproof pen. Make sure all the corners are true right angles. This rectangle should be larger than the embroidery, as it is there to provide straight lines to follow when pinning out the fabric.

2 Lay the paper on the pinboard and cover it with the sheet of plastic.

3 Trim any excess fabric from the edges of the embroidery, leaving enough turnings, 20mm (¾in) minimum, to allow for the drawing pins.

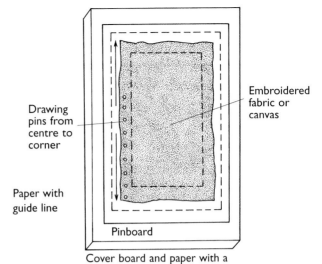

Drawing pins from centre to corner

Embroidered fabric or canvas

Paper with guide line

Pinboard

Cover board and paper with a sheet of transparent plastic

Fig 14.4 **Blocking a completed piece of canvaswork into shape.**

4 With a small damp cloth or sponge, dampen the embroidery and the surrounding canvas or linen.

5 Lay the embroidery within the paper rectangle and begin pinning the fabric to the board, from the middle of one side to the corner, stretching the fabric slightly as you work. Use the line on the paper as a guide (*see* Fig 14.4).

6 Return to the middle of the side and work towards the other corner in the same way.

7 Repeat the process along the opposite sides.

8 Repeat again on the two remaining sides.

9 Leave the piece to dry naturally, lying flat in an even temperature.

10 When completely dry, remove the pins. Occasionally, if the piece was very badly distorted, the process may need to be repeated.

Mitred corners

Working a mitred corner will help to cut down unnecessary bulk.

Working method

1 Trim the seam allowance.

2 Cut a small amount from the corner of the fabric (*see* Fig 14.5A).

3 Fold the corner down diagonally.

4 Fold the adjacent sides once, and then again to form a hem (*see* Fig 14.5B and C). Secure with tiny hemming stitches.

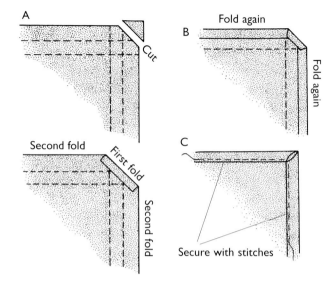

Fig 14.5 **Making a mitred corner.**

Methods of fastening on

The old rule that 'thou shalt not start with a knot' derives from a time when most embroidered articles had to be laundered, and a knot would unravel in the washing process.

With miniatures, which are unlikely to need repeated washing, it is *sometimes* an advantage to begin with a small knot. However, the best method, once some stitching has been worked, is to secure the beginning of the thread into the back of the existing stitching.

Backstitch

A stitch that makes a line.

Bring the needle up through from the back of the fabric and take it down again to give the length of stitch required. Bring the needle up through the fabric again, the length of a stitch away from the previous stitch (at A). Take the needle back through the fabric, next to the previous stitch (B).

When complete, fasten off into the back of the stitches.

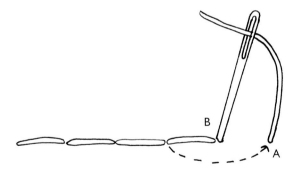

Blanket or buttonhole stitch

This stitch can form an edging, a row of stitching, or be radiated to form a flower effect.

Bring the needle up through the fabric at A, and take it down at B, a little to one side of A. Pick up a stitch (B to C) to give the desired length and direction. Bring the needle back through, making sure the thread is behind the needle. Continue in this way (D to E) keeping the thread behind the needle.

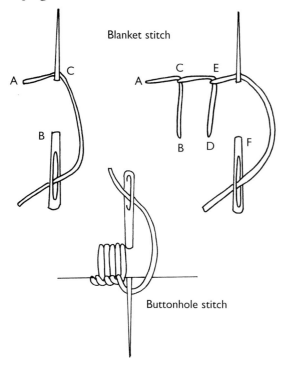

Blanket stitch

Buttonhole stitch

When complete, fasten off into the back of the stitches.

Buttonhole stitch is worked in the same way, but with the stitches very close together.

Couching

This method is used to lay a thread on the surface of the fabric, which is stitched down with a second, finer thread.

Bring the thread to be laid through from the back of the fabric. In another needle, bring the sewing thread through from the back, immediately beside the first thread (A), and take a stitch over the first thread. Continue to secure the first thread in this manner, at the same time moving the first thread, if necessary, to form the shape or line required.

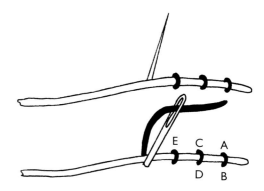

Fasten the sewing thread off behind the stitching, then take the first thread through to the back and fasten it off.

Cross stitch

The diagram shows the method for working a row of cross stitch by making the first half of each stitch all the way along the row and then working the second half on the way back along the row.

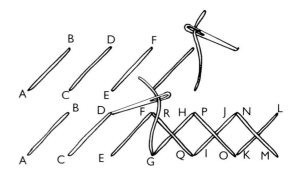

Individual crosses can be worked by making the two stitches immediately one after the other. Which method you choose will depend on the design.

Fasten off in the back of the stitching.

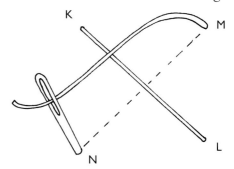

Cushion stitch

Cushion stitch forms a square of diagonal stitches. Each alternate square has the stitches sloping in the opposite direction.

The first stitch is worked diagonally over one thread, the second over two, and the third over three. The fourth stitch is worked over two threads and the final stitch over one, thus forming a square.

To begin working the next square, bring the needle up at K as shown, and take it down at L.

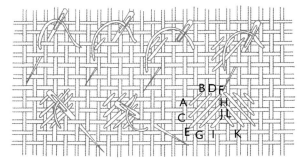

First stitch   Second stitch   Third stitch   Fourth stitch

Darning

This stitch is worked only on evenweave fabrics or canvas and produces a regular pattern. A tapestry needle must be used.

Fasten off into the back of the stitching.

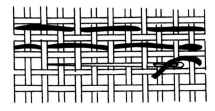

Detached chain stitch

This stitch is useful for flowers and leaves. A short stitch produces a rounded shape while a longer stitch produces a narrower shape.

Bring the needle up through the back of the fabric (A), then take it down as close as possible to the same point (B). Bring the needle up again at C, making a stitch of the length required, and looping the thread under the needle. Pull the thread through and take a small stitch over the loop to secure it (D).

When complete, fasten off in the back of the stitching.

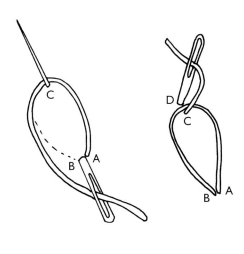

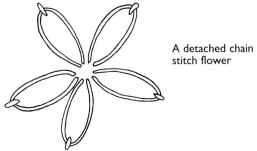

A detached chain stitch flower

Feather stitch

Bring the needle through from the back of the fabric and make a stitch at an angle, forming a triangle, with the thread under the needle. Draw the thread through.

Continiue taking stitches at an angle, first to one side, then to the other.

When the required number of stitches are completed, take a small stitch over the last loop to secure.

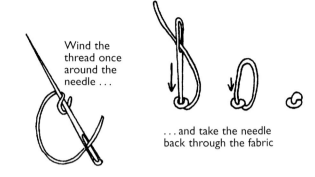

Wind the thread once around the needle . . .

. . . and take the needle back through the fabric

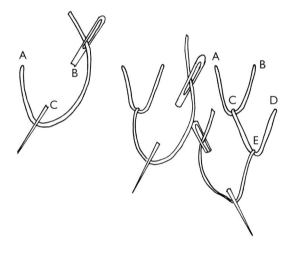

Hemming

This stitch is used to secure a hem. Turn the edge of the fabric over as desired. Pick up a little of the fabric and the turned hem and draw the thread through, repeating until the entire hem is secure. Only a tiny stitch should show on the right side of the fabric, so it is an advantage to use a very fine needle.

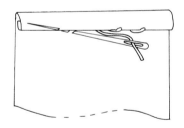

French knot

This stitch can be used alone or clustered together.

Bring the needle through from the back of the fabric and wind the thread once around the needle. Take the point of the needle back through the fabric, very close to where the thread was brought through to the front. Draw the thread through to the back of the fabric. When complete, this will form a neat, compact knot.

Herringbone stitch

Herringbone stitch is generally used to give a decorative border, but can also be used as a filling stitch.

Bring the needle through from the back of the fabric and make a diagonal stitch. Bring the needle back through a short space away horizontally. Make another diagonal stitch which crosses over the first. Continue until complete.

Fasten off into the back of the stitching.

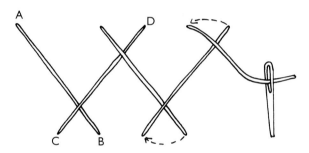

Holbein stitch

A reversible double running stitch used on collars, cuffs and where both sides of the fabric would be seen.

Laid work

Bring the needle through to the front of the fabric at the end of one of the trellis lines. Take the needle back through at the other end of the trellis line. Continue as shown until all the lines have been laid in one direction.

Repeat the process, placing the second layer of threads.

Finally, with sewing thread, work along the lines of the trellis placing a tiny stitch over the places where the laid threads cross.

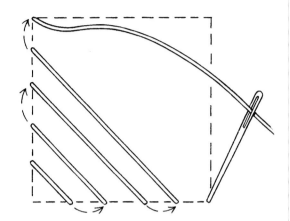

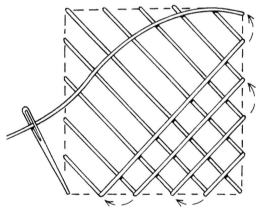

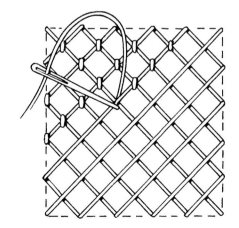

155

Running stitch

This stitch is basically the same as darning, but it is worked on a plain fabric and not counted. It can be used for outlining and in quilting.

The needle is simply taken in and out of the fabric to form the line or shape required.

If the stitch is used for quilting, a smaller stitch can be obtained by stab stitching. Take the needle through the fabrics and draw the thread through, then, in a second movement, bring the needle and thread back through the fabrics again. Work each stitch in two movements.

Length of space is equivalent to length of stitch

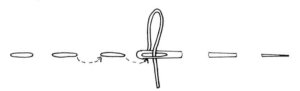

Satin stitch

This stitch is used as a filling for small areas. Bring the needle through from the back of the fabric, on the outline of the shape. Take the needle back through the fabric on the opposite side of the shape. Continue to place stitches next to one another in this manner until the shape is filled. Fasten off into the back of the stitching.

Seeding stitches

Seeding is an effect created by short, straight stitches scattered at various angles. Traditionally, two stitches were used side by side, but for miniature work one is sufficient.

Straight stitch

Straight stitch is the most basic and versatile embroidery stitch. It can be used for tiny leaves or flowers. It is simply a single stitch which can be of any length, and used side by side or set at an angle to radiate.

Bring the needle through from the back of the fabric and take it down again to make a stitch of the length required. Continue laying stitches in this way to give the effect that you require.

Tent stitch

This stitch is used on an evenweave fabric or canvas. By using tent stitch, rather than half cross stitch, the stitches can be worked in any direction and will look exactly the same on the front. Tent Stitch also prevents the thread from slipping behind the weave of the fabric and disappearing.

The top diagram shows the placing of the needle. The numbered diagram gives the sequence for different directions. Bring the needle up through the odd numbers and take the needle back down through the even numbers.

When rows are worked next to one another, the same holes are used as the previous row. Do not leave a thread of canvas empty in between.

Tent stitch can also slope from top left to bottom right.

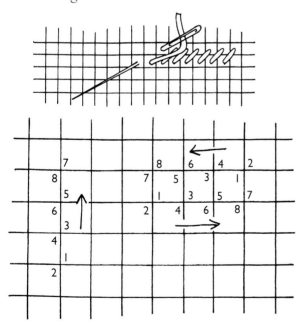

Sources of information

Museums

Most large towns and cities have a museum with a display of decorative arts, which will include embroidered items. Many will cover social history, showing the way in which people lived and the artefacts they used in their everyday lives. Some museums will have authentic room settings with furnishings of a particular period. These will provide valuable general information.

If you have a specific question, it is best to write to the curator in advance, stating exactly what you wish to know. A short list of clear questions will almost always bring a prompt response, but a general 'Tell me all you know about beds/chairs/Tudor houses/etc' will rarely get a reply.

In most countries, a list of museums and historical houses is published, usually updated every couple of years or so. Libraries will have copies, or lists of their own, and sometimes a section devoted to local history.

The brief list that follows is a starting point, indicating museums which have collections of Tudor and Stuart historical embroidery and, in some cases, furnishings.

United Kingdom and Ireland

Geffrye Museum
Kingsland Road
London E2 8EA
020 7739 8368/9893

Room settings.

The Embroiderers' Guild
Apartment 41
Hampton Court Palace
East Molesey
Surrey KT8 9AU
020 8943 1229

By appointment only.
Historical embroidery.
The Guild has branches
throughout the UK and
Ireland, the USA, Canada
and Australia.

Victoria and Albert Museum
Cromwell Road
London SW7
020 7942 2000

Embroidery, costume and furniture.

Bowes Museum
Barnard Castle
Co. Durham DL12 8NP
01833 690606

Embroidery, costume and furnishings.

Fitzwilliam Museum
Trumpington Street
Cambridge
Cambridgeshire CB2 1RB
01223 332900

Embroidery, mostly samplers.

Guildford Museum
Castle Arch
Guildford
Surrey GU1 3SX
01483 444750

Some embroidery.

Maidstone Museum and Art Gallery
St Faith's Street
Maidstone
Kent ME14 1LH
01622 754497

Embroidery and furnishings.

Whitworth Art Gallery
University of Manchester
Oxford Road
Manchester
Greater Manchester M15 6ER
0161 275 7450

Fabrics and furnishings.

Museum of Costume and Textiles
51 Castle Gate
Nottingham
Nottinghamshire NG1 6AF
0115 915 3500/5555

Costume, embroidery and lace.

York Castle Museum
The Eye of York
York
Yorkshire YO1 9RY
01904 653611

Room settings.

Royal Museum
Chambers Street
Edinburgh EH1 1JF
Scotland
0131 225 7534

Embroideries.

The Burrell Collection
Pollok Country Park
2060 Pollokshaws Road
Glasgow G43 1AT
Scotland
0141 287 2550

Embroideries and tapestries.

Ulster Folk & Transport Museum
153 Bangor Road
Cultra
Holywood
Co. Down BT18 0EU
Northern Ireland
028 9042 8428

Textiles and crafts.

Ulster Museum
Botanic Gardens
Stranmillis Road
Belfast BT9 5AB
Northern Ireland
02890 383000

Costume and lace.

National Museum of Ireland
Kildare Street and
7–9 Merrion Row
  and Merrion Street
Dublin 2
Republic of Ireland
003531 6777 444

Decorative arts and lace.

United States of America and Canada

Museum of Fine Arts
465 Huntington Avenue
Boston
Massachusetts 02115
617 267 9300

Large collection of textiles.

The Art Institute of Chicago
Michigan Avenue
    at Adams Street
Chicago
Illinois 60603
312 443 3600

Large collection of textiles.

The Brooklyn Museum
200 Eastern Parkway
Brooklyn
New York City
New York 11238
718 638 5000

Costume, bed hangings and
window hangings.

The Metropolitan Museum of Art
1000 Fifth Avenue
5th Avenue at 82nd Street
New York City
New York 10028
212 879 5500

Costume and embroideries.

Philadelphia Museum of Art
Box 7646
Philadelphia
Pennsylvania 19101
215 763 8100

American and English
embroideries.

National Museum of History and Technology
Smithsonian Institution
14th Street and Constitution
Avenue
Washington DC 20560
202 357 2700

Coverlets and embroideries.

Royal Ontario Museum
100 Queens Park
Toronto
Ontario M5S 2C6
416 586 5549

Large collection of embroidery and
lace.

Note: Many Canadian museums
specialize in folk textiles, but may
have small collections of
embroidery.

Historic houses

These houses, which are well documented in books, magazines and libraries, are a good source of reference. Some are dedicated and restored to one particular era, but many have been added to over the centuries.

In most countries there are heritage organizations to care for these estates and houses, such as the National Trust and English Heritage in the United Kingdom.

Usually, a booklet or postcards are available.

Books

Information and illustrations can be found in books on embroidery, interior decoration, restoring period houses, furniture and decorative art styles. There are many specialist periodicals available covering these areas. Your local reference library, or a browse in a large book shop, are good starting points.

The brief list which follows includes some books which may be out of print, but can be seen at libraries or purchased from secondhand book dealers.

Artley, Alexandra (Editor),
Putting Back the Style,
Ward Lock, London, UK, 1988
ISBN 07063 6708 1

Benn, Elizabeth (Editor),
Treasures from the Embroiderers' Guild Collection, David & Charles, Devon, UK, 1991
ISBN 07153 9829 6

Johnson, Pauline,
Three Hundred Years of Embroidery, 1600–1900, Wakefield Press in association with the Embroiderers' Guild of South Australia and The Embroiderers' Guild, Hampton Court Palace, Surrey, UK, 1987
ISBN 0949268 81X

King, Donald and **Levy**, Santina,
The Victoria and Albert Museum's Textile Collection, Embroidery in Britain from 1200 to 1750, V&A Museum, UK, 1993
ISBN 085533 6501

Miller, Judith and Martin,
Period Details, Mitchell Beazley, London, UK, 1988
ISBN 085533 6501

Swain, Margaret,
Scottish Embroidery, Medieval to Modern, B. T. Batsford Ltd, London, UK, 1986
ISBN 07134 4638 2

Vince, John,
The Country House, How it Worked, John Murray (Publishers) Ltd, London, UK, 1991
ISBN 07195 4769 5

Warner, Pamela,
Embroidery: A History,
B. T. Batsford Ltd, London, UK, 1991
ISBN 07134 61063

About the author

Pamela Warner's interest in embroidery began in the mid-1950s with her studies for a National Design Diploma (NDD) in fashion – which included embroidery – at Bromley College of Art.

After a career in banking and computing, followed by marriage and a family, Pamela rediscovered creative embroidery at an evening class. She went on to qualify and by 1979 was teaching embroidery for Bromley Adult Education and the Inner London Education Authority (ILEA). During the early 1980s she became involved as a tutor for City and Guilds embroidery classes at Bromley, and eventually took on full responsibility for the course. This continues to be her main occupation, along with working as an external verifier for the City and Guilds examination board. In 1999, Pamela formulated a syllabus for City and Guilds, enabling embroiderers to achieve a certificate in Miniature Embroidery.

Pamela discovered dolls' houses in 1989. She began with a ready-made house and a kit, but was soon frustrated with the small rooms. In order to learn the craft herself, she went on a Dolls' House Holiday, with Peter Alden, and was so impressed with the results that she keeps returning.

Pamela's work as a professional embroiderer has been exhibited widely, and she has undertaken many commissions for ecclesiastic and secular pieces. She has also spent 15 years restoring and conserving embroideries for Westminster Abbey and other churches.

This is Pamela's fourth book, following *Embroidery: A History; Miniature Embroidery for the Victorian Dolls' House;* and *Miniature Embroidery for the Georgian Dolls' House*, as well as a series of booklets on the history of embroidery.

Index

GMC Publications

WOODCARVING

The Art of the Woodcarver	*GMC Publications*
Carving Architectural Detail in Wood: The Classical Tradition	*Frederick Wilbur*
Carving Birds & Beasts	*GMC Publications*
Carving the Human Figure: Studies in Wood and Stone	*Dick Onians*
Carving Nature: Wildlife Studies in Wood	*Frank Fox-Wilson*
Carving Realistic Birds	*David Tippey*
Decorative Woodcarving	*Jeremy Williams*
Elements of Woodcarving	*Chris Pye*
Essential Woodcarving Techniques	*Dick Onians*
Lettercarving in Wood: A Practical Course	*Chris Pye*
Making & Using Working Drawings for Realistic Model Animals	*Basil F. Fordham*
Power Tools for Woodcarving	*David Tippey*
Relief Carving in Wood: A Practical Introduction	*Chris Pye*
Understanding Woodcarving	*GMC Publications*
Understanding Woodcarving in the Round	*GMC Publications*
Useful Techniques for Woodcarvers	*GMC Publications*
Wildfowl Carving – Volume 1	*Jim Pearce*
Wildfowl Carving – Volume 2	*Jim Pearce*
Woodcarving: A Complete Course	*Ron Butterfield*
Woodcarving: A Foundation Course	*Zoë Gertner*
Woodcarving for Beginners	*GMC Publications*
Woodcarving Tools & Equipment Test Reports	*GMC Publications*
Woodcarving Tools, Materials & Equipment	*Chris Pye*

WOODTURNING

Adventures in Woodturning	*David Springett*
Bert Marsh: Woodturner	*Bert Marsh*
Bowl Turning Techniques Masterclass	*Tony Boase*
Colouring Techniques for Woodturners	*Jan Sanders*
Contemporary Turned Wood: New Perspectives in a Rich Tradition	*Ray Leier, Jan Peters & Kevin Wallace*
The Craftsman Woodturner	*Peter Child*
Decorating Turned Wood: The Maker's Eye	*Liz & Michael O'Donnell*
Decorative Techniques for Woodturners	*Hilary Bowen*
Fun at the Lathe	*R.C. Bell*
Illustrated Woodturning Techniques	*John Hunnex*
Intermediate Woodturning Projects	*GMC Publications*
Keith Rowley's Woodturning Projects	*Keith Rowley*
Making Screw Threads in Wood	*Fred Holder*
Turned Boxes: 50 Designs	*Chris Stott*
Turning Green Wood	*Michael O'Donnell*
Turning Miniatures in Wood	*John Sainsbury*
Turning Pens and Pencils	*Kip Christensen & Rex Burningham*
Understanding Woodturning	*Ann & Bob Phillips*
Useful Techniques for Woodturners	*GMC Publications*
Useful Woodturning Projects	*GMC Publications*
Woodturning: Bowls, Platters, Hollow Forms, Vases, Vessels, Bottles, Flasks, Tankards, Plates	*GMC Publications*
Woodturning: A Foundation Course (New Edition)	*Keith Rowley*
Woodturning: A Fresh Approach	*Robert Chapman*
Woodturning: An Individual Approach	*Dave Regester*
Woodturning: A Source Book of Shapes	*John Hunnex*
Woodturning Jewellery	*Hilary Bowen*
Woodturning Masterclass	*Tony Boase*
Woodturning Techniques	*GMC Publications*
Woodturning Tools & Equipment Test Reports	*GMC Publications*
Woodturning Wizardry	*David Springett*

WOODWORKING

Advanced Scrollsaw Projects	*GMC Publications*
Beginning Picture Marquetry	*Lawrence Threadgold*
Bird Boxes and Feeders for the Garden	*Dave Mackenzie*
Complete Woodfinishing	*Ian Hosker*
David Charlesworth's Furniture-Making Techniques	
	David Charlesworth
David Charlesworth's Furniture-Making Techniques –	
Volume 2	*David Charlesworth*
The Encyclopedia of Joint Making	*Terrie Noll*
Furniture-Making Projects for the Wood Craftsman	
	GMC Publications
Furniture-Making Techniques for the Wood Craftsman	
	GMC Publications
Furniture Projects	*Rod Wales*
Furniture Restoration (Practical Crafts)	*Kevin Jan Bonner*
Furniture Restoration: A Professional at Work	*John Lloyd*
Furniture Restoration and Repair for Beginners	
	Kevin Jan Bonner
Furniture Restoration Workshop	*Kevin Jan Bonner*
Green Woodwork	*Mike Abbott*
The History of Furniture	*Michael Huntley*
Intarsia: 30 Patterns for the Scrollsaw	*John Everett*
Kevin Ley's Furniture Projects	*Kevin Ley*
Making & Modifying Woodworking Tools	*Jim Kingshott*
Making Chairs and Tables	*GMC Publications*
Making Chairs and Tables – Volume 2	*GMC Publications*
Making Classic English Furniture	*Paul Richardson*
Making Heirloom Boxes	*Peter Lloyd*
Making Little Boxes from Wood	*John Bennett*
Making Screw Threads in Wood	*Fred Holder*
Making Shaker Furniture	*Barry Jackson*
Making Woodwork Aids and Devices	*Robert Wearing*
Mastering the Router	*Ron Fox*
Minidrill: Fifteen Projects	*John Everett*
Pine Furniture Projects for the Home	*Dave Mackenzie*
Practical Scrollsaw Patterns	*John Everett*
Router Magic: Jigs, Fixtures and Tricks to	
Unleash your Router's Full Potential	*Bill Hylton*
Router Tips & Techniques	*GMC Publications*
Routing: A Workshop Handbook	*Anthony Bailey*
Routing for Beginners	*Anthony Bailey*
The Scrollsaw: Twenty Projects	*John Everett*
Sharpening: The Complete Guide	*Jim Kingshott*
Sharpening Pocket Reference Book	*Jim Kingshott*
Simple Scrollsaw Projects	*GMC Publications*

Space-Saving Furniture Projects	*Dave Mackenzie*
Stickmaking: A Complete Course	*Andrew Jones & Clive George*
Stickmaking Handbook	*Andrew Jones & Clive George*
Storage Projects for the Router	*GMC Publications*
Test Reports: The Router and Furniture & Cabinetmaking	
	GMC Publications
Veneering: A Complete Course	*Ian Hosker*
Veneering Handbook	*Ian Hosker*
Woodfinishing Handbook (Practical Crafts)	*Ian Hosker*
Woodworking with the Router: Professional	
Router Techniques any Woodworker can Use	
	Bill Hylton & Fred Matlack
The Workshop	*Jim Kingshott*

UPHOLSTERY

The Upholsterer's Pocket Reference Book	*David James*
Upholstery: A Complete Course (Revised Edition)	
	David James
Upholstery Restoration	*David James*
Upholstery Techniques & Projects	*David James*
Upholstery Tips and Hints	*David James*

TOYMAKING

Restoring Rocking Horses	*Clive Green & Anthony Dew*
Scrollsaw Toy Projects	*Ivor Carlyle*
Scrollsaw Toys for All Ages	*Ivor Carlyle*

DOLLS' HOUSES AND MINIATURES

1/12 Scale Character Figures for the Dolls' House	
	James Carrington
Architecture for Dolls' Houses	*Joyce Percival*
The Authentic Georgian Dolls' House	*Brian Long*
A Beginners' Guide to the Dolls' House Hobby	*Jean Nisbett*
Celtic, Medieval and Tudor Wall Hangings in	
1/12 Scale Needlepoint	*Sandra Whitehead*
The Complete Dolls' House Book	*Jean Nisbett*
The Dolls' House 1/24 Scale: A Complete Introduction	
	Jean Nisbett
Dolls' House Accessories, Fixtures and Fittings	
	Andrea Barham
Dolls' House Bathrooms: Lots of Little Loos	*Patricia King*
Dolls' House Fireplaces and Stoves	*Patricia King*
Dolls' House Makeovers	*Jean Nisbett*
Dolls' House Window Treatments	*Eve Harwood*
Easy to Make Dolls' House Accessories	*Andrea Barham*

CRAFTS

GARDENING

PHOTOGRAPHY

VIDEOS

Drop-in and Pinstuffed Seats	*David James*
Stuffover Upholstery	*David James*
Elliptical Turning	*David Springett*
Woodturning Wizardry	*David Springett*
Turning Between Centres: The Basics	*Dennis White*
Turning Bowls	*Dennis White*
Boxes, Goblets and Screw Threads	*Dennis White*
Novelties and Projects	*Dennis White*
Classic Profiles	*Dennis White*
Twists and Advanced Turning	*Dennis White*
Sharpening the Professional Way	*Jim Kingshott*
Sharpening Turning & Carving Tools	*Jim Kingshott*
Bowl Turning	*John Jordan*
Hollow Turning	*John Jordan*
Woodturning: A Foundation Course	*Keith Rowley*
Carving a Figure: The Female Form	*Ray Gonzalez*
The Router: A Beginner's Guide	*Alan Goodsell*
The Scroll Saw: A Beginner's Guide	*John Burke*

MAGAZINES

WOODTURNING ◆ WOODCARVING
FURNITURE & CABINETMAKING
THE ROUTER ◆ WOODWORKING
THE DOLLS' HOUSE MAGAZINE
WATER GARDENING
OUTDOOR PHOTOGRAPHY
BLACK & WHITE PHOTOGRAPHY
BUSINESS MATTERS

The above represents a full list of all titles currently
published or scheduled to be published.
All are available direct from the Publishers or through
bookshops, newsagents and specialist retailers.

To place an order, or to obtain a complete catalogue,
contact:

**GMC Publications
Castle Place
166 High Street
Lewes, East Sussex BN7 1XU
United Kingdom**

Tel: 01273 488005   Fax: 01273 478606

Email: pubs@thegmcgroup.com

Orders by credit card are accepted